Philip Howard Colomb

THE DANGERS

OF THE

MODERN RULE OF THE ROAD

AT SEA

AND THE MANOEUVRING POWERS OF SHIPS
AS AFFECTING COLLISION

Elibron Classics
www.elibron.com

Elibron Classics series.

ISBN 0-543-97944-X (paperback)
ISBN 0-543-97943-1 (hardcover)

This Elibron Classics Replica Edition is an unabridged facsimile
of the edition published in 1885 by J. Griffin and Co., Portsmouth.

THE DANGERS OF THE
MODERN RULE OF THE ROAD AT SEA.

THE DANGERS

OF THE

MODERN RULE OF THE ROAD

AT SEA,

AND THE MANŒUVRING POWERS OF SHIPS AS AFFECTING COLLISION.

BY

CAPTAIN P. H. COLOMB, R.N.,

JOINT-AUTHOR OF "THE LAW OF PORT-HELM," AUTHOR OF "OUR PERIL AFLOAT," ETC.

1885.

J. GRIFFIN AND CO.,

(*Publishers by Appointment to H. M. The Queen, and H.R.H. The Duke of Edinburgh,*)

2, THE HARD, PORTSMOUTH.

Griffin and Co.,
2, The Hard, Portsmouth.

CONTENTS.

ADDRESS.

To the Right Hon. the Earl of Aberdeen, Chairman of the Royal Commission on the Loss of Life at Sea.

My Lord,

I observe that the terms of the Royal Commission over which you preside, include inquiry into any other causes of loss of life at sea beside those to which your attention is more particularly directed. It is on this ground that I venture to address to you this little work on one cause of loss of life, to which my attention has for many years past been earnestly given. I may flatter myself in having urged and advocated most of the improvements in the regulations for avoiding collisions at sea, which have been introduced of late years—notably the limitation of what has been called "the law of port helm" for steamers, and its entire abolition for sailing vessels, and also with reference to improved fitting of the anti-collision, or coloured side-lights.

While, however, something has been done towards mitigating the dangers of collisions, the numbers and disastrous character of these accidents is enough to show that much more remains to be done.

The course of my inquiries into this subject has now extended over some eighteen years, and has led me to go deeply and largely into the two departments of fact, whence alone—as I believe—reliable grounds for inquiry can be drawn: namely, into the circumstances attending actual collisions, and into the powers of manœuvring which ships really possess for avoiding them.

In the former inquiry I suppose I must have examined about a thousand cases; and in the latter I have made several hundreds of experiments. Recent official employment embraced this latter experimental inquiry, and I have by me the experimental measurement of the manœuvring powers of a considerable number of H.M. ships, varying in type from the 10,000-ton Ironclad to the little Steam-Pinnace.

Any conclusions, therefore, at which I may have arrived, will not be erroneous on account of lack of data; but if they are so, will remain wrong in spite of the data.

From an original acceptance of the common belief that collisions at sea were generally due to the negligence, carelessuess, or disobedience of seamen, I have risen to the conviction that the main cause is much deeper. I am satisfied that the preventible collisions —and most collisions at sea are preventible—are chiefly due to an ignorance of the subject which has been fostered by the modern regulations, and the authoritative and other glosses which have been placed upon them.

Except incidentally, and by way of criticism on published glosses, I do not on this occasion go beyond the general principles which ought to govern any Rule of the Road at sea, and the way in which our modern rules fall short of them. There is a great deal to be said, *pro* and *con*, on most of the existing regulations; but it is of less utility to consider matters of detail before general principles are accepted.

I prefer making specific charges against the principles of the existing rules, and bending my energies to their proof, to embarking in discussions which I have found to be rather one-sided, in the absence of common groundwork of belief.

The charges, for convenience, may be formulated thus:

(1) That whereas an admirable and efficient system of anti-collision lights has been adopted by the ships of all nations, the law is so framed as to ignore the signals such lights convey; and even, in cases, to order disobedience to them.

(2) That whereas the sole function of a Rule of the Road at sea ought to be the settlement of the question, which ship of any pair approaching each other, should have the right to pass ahead of, or in front of, the other?—the modern rules neglect this question altogether, and busy themselves with complexities which ought to be, and used to be, left out of view.

It is proper to point out that the main contents of the first chapter of this little work, in somewhat varied matter and manner, were brought by me before the Thames Traffic Committee, which sat subsequent to the lamentable loss of the 600 lives in the *Princess Alice.* My long examination, and some—but not the most important—of the papers put in by me, are published in the Report. But at that time I was possessed of only a little of the experimental data now at my disposal. I could then only infer what I can now demonstrate, and the Committee—perhaps naturally—concluded that they had a right to assume that the single ship I was able to work with was of so peculiar a character that she could not be used as an exemplar. I should probably not be writing now on this subject were I not able to show by hundreds of experiments, with varied types, that my inferences were quite correct.

My chief aim, however, in venturing to address these remarks to you is to point out that while the rules are in the unsatisfactory conditions described, there has never yet been held any inquiry into their working. Nor has there ever been, into any collision, the sort of inquiry which is held every day into railway or colliery accidents. The rules have, in all cases, been drawn up apart from data furnished by actual collision, and being drawn up and made law, they are treated in all cases of collision as not subject to inquiry. Yet every collision is due to fact and law in combination. Ships cannot approach to make a collision without obeying or disobeying some rule, but the rule is never on trial. In the case of the port helm rule, for instance—once universal, now limited for steamers meeting steamers under particular circumstances, and abolished in all other cases—it was not until Captain Brent and I in the year 1867 were able to show how large a per-centage of the collisions occurring was directly due to obedience to this law, that a movement was set on foot with the results described. But in all the inquiries, the law was necessarily held to be right, without the admission of a question. It is still so. If a ship authorized to keep her course, runs down another ship while doing so, the inquiry must stop at her proof of authority so far as she and the law she has obeyed are concerned. It is not open to discussion whether the law she obeyed is a good and a safe one, or whether, like the law of port helm, it was so dangerous that it ought never to have been framed as it stood.

A remarkable instance of this singular state of affairs is seen in the Report of the Thames Traffic Committee already alluded to. Two steamers came into collision in the Thames under circumstances involving the leading principles of the established Rule of the Road at sea. The *Princess Alice* sank and drowned some 600 excursionists on board her. There was considerable excitement and feeling, and the Government appointed a strong committee to inquire into the rules under which traffic was carried on in the Thames. Had the accident been a railway or a colliery accident, a committee of inquiry would have gone closely and directly into every detail relating, however remotely, to the accident. It would have been understood that the Report must either say that nothing in the way of legislation could have prevented the accident, or else must present a project of law, having for its object the prevention of future accidents of the kind.

The loss of the *Princess Alice*, however, formed no part of the inquiry or Report of the Thames Traffic Committee. The subject of the particular accident not being considered before the Committee, came in only for incidental mention; and then by permission.

The difficulty I understand to be, that in a collision case some one is always on his trial. There is no such thing as inquiry preliminary to trial; and hence obedience or disobedience to the law is the only point at issue.

But a Royal Commission inquiring into causes of loss of life at sea, may be—in my conception at least—free from the bonds which have hampered other tribunals, and in suggesting the contents of the following pages as a proper foundation for inquiry, I am, I hope not wrongly, expressing my belief.

I have the honour to be,

My Lord,

Your Lordship's obedient Servant,

P. H. Colomb.

THE DANGERS OF THE

MODERN RULE OF THE ROAD AT SEA.

CHAPTER I.

FAULTY PRINCIPLES.

ARTICLE 15 of the steering and sailing rules, orders that "if two ships under steam are meeting end on, or nearly end on, so as to involve risk of collision, each shall alter her course to starboard, so that each may pass on the port side of the other." *

From 1854 to 1863 this order to 'port the helm' was the only rule for British ships of all classes, no matter how they were approaching, so long as there was 'risk of collision.' I am happy in having assisted in banishing the rule altogether for sailing ships, and in restricting the meaning of 'end-on, or nearly end-on,' to presumably narrow limits for steamers. I hope to assist in the removal of all that is now left of this 'port helm' rule.

For I will point out that before this rule can be obeyed, there must be concurrence of opinion between two officers who can neither hear nor see each other, and one of whom may not even see the ship of the other, on two distinct points; namely:—as to whether there is 'risk of collision,' and whether *each* ship is 'end-on, or nearly end-on' to the other, and I will ask whether it can be anything but dangerous to retain a rule which requires an improbability to set it in motion?

* The regulations are printed in full at the end of this book as an Appendix.

I need not add that ships do often thus come into collision, from one officer imagining a concurrence which the other does not admit.

But I will go further, and state that the explanatory clauses, added in some hopes of aiding a concurrence of opinion, contain in them a direct and palpable incentive to collision.

The second explanatory clause points out that the rule applies at night when *each* ship is in a position to see both the side-lights of the other. That is, in other words, it is the mariner's duty to put his helm to port, and to turn his steamer to starboard (or to the right), whenever he sees, nearly ahead of his own ship, the red and green lights of an approaching steamer. If the second ship sees the red and green lights of the first nearly ahead, and obeys the same direction, no doubt all would go well. But so would all go well if the second ship neglected to do anything whatever, and simply continued her course. So therefore would all go well if the second ship had never seen the first at all.*

Referring to Fig. 1, we have a steamer X steering towards A, seeing the red and green lights of a steamer Y only 5° from being 'right ahead,' and which is steering, as it happens, towards B; being therefore 'nearly end-on' to X, X is bound by law to alter her course towards C, by which she evidently clears the path of Y, and leaves her free to go on. If Y happens to see both the red and green lights of X, and obeys the law by altering her course towards D, no harm comes of it; but it is manifestly a work of supererogation, as her original path has been cleared for her by the action of X.

But it very seldom happens at sea that the red and green lights come into view together. It is a physical impossibility, for instance, to get and to keep the lights equally visible in the varying conditions of the atmosphere. The 'yawing' motion of the ship, either designed or undesigned, shows green added to red; or red added to green; and then green becomes subtracted from red, or

* This has been fully admitted ever since 1863, as then no rule was introduced for steamers meeting sailing vessels 'end-on, or nearly end-on;' and now it is admitted for sailing vessels meeting sailing vessels under like conditions. The understanding in all these cases is that one vessel only need alter course.

red becomes subtracted from green. The facts of the case being that while red by itself, or green by itself is visible over 112½° of the horizon, red and green together, ought in strict accordance with the law, to be so arranged as *never* to be visible to one pair of eyes. And even as now generally fitted, are visible together only over a very few degrees of the horizon.

But if red becomes added to green, in a ship nearly ahead of another, it is generally a clear signal, that the first ship is altering her course to starboard (or to her own right), and it is a safety signal to the second ship, absolving her from the necessity of taking any steps—so far as natural, apart from legal, requirements are concerned. It is, however, a very distinct signal forbidding the second ship to put her helm to starboard (to turn to her left), for that is to run straight into danger. If green is next seen to be subtracted from red, it is a confirmation of the safety signal, that the ships will clear each other. As in Fig. 1, it is quite possible that Y may at first see only the green light of X, and if she next sees red added to green, it is almost a certain signal that X is altering her course towards C. If, then, Y sees further, green subtracted from red, it is an absolute confirmation of the previous signal.

If, however, green is added to red in a ship nearly ahead of another, it is generally a signal that the first ship is altering her course to port (or to her own left). It is, equally with the former case, a safety signal to the second ship, absolving her from any natural necessity to alter her own course, but warning her distinctly *not* to turn to the right, because that is to run straight into the danger.

But here the law steps in, and orders that the second ship *shall* turn to the right, in quite as distinct terms as the coloured lights order that she *shall not.*

If we turn to Fig. 2 we shall find X and Y 'nearly end-on' as before, the only difference being that X is a little to the right of Y's path, whereas she was a little to the left of it in Fig. 1. It is quite possible that X should see only the green light of Y; and without some closer observation than is generally practicable at night, it is quite possible she might think it not on her port bow.*

* This is almost a platitude to the student of actual cases of collision.

Some starboard helm is under such circumstances very generally employed by seamen in order not to pass too close to the approaching ship. The danger of the movement is by no means admitted, and has never, I believe, been held to be a thing improper in itself. Indeed we might have assumed X to steer a course really clear of Y, starboard side to starboard side, without altering the conditions of the argument. By choice then, and as a measure of precaution, X starboards her helm, and turns to the left. In doing so, she will, to the view of Y, add the green to the red, and thus make the signal which by law Y must obey.

Each ship is in such a position as to see both side-lights of the other, and Article 15 declares to Y that she '*shall* alter her course to starboard.' She does so, and collision occurs at the point O, because Y knew what X could not.*

The lights being fitted generally so that they can both be seen together—if only over a very small arc of the horizon—it unfortunately happens that ships very often do obey the law, to their own or their neighbours' destruction—too often indeed to their mutual destruction. But in all such cases the blame is always taken off the shoulders of the law, and placed on those of the mariner in the first ship (X); who from many circumstances, for which he is in no way responsible, may never have seen until too late, or may never have seen at all, the signal which would have ordered him to turn to his left.†

* There is a very important point in reference to collisions of this kind, which has never, so far as I am aware, been authoritatively noticed. It is this: X having starboarded a little as a precautionary measure simply, would generally steady after a very slight change of course. Y obeying the law, and expecting safety from it, will not at first give much helm. She may just give enough to continually keep from X the sight of the red light until it is too late for X to render obedience to such a signal. X being just on Y's starboard bow, may have speed enough to remain on Y's starboard bow till the disaster occurs. There are instances of this.

† I may quote a few cases in point. The *Bombay* saw both coloured lights of the *Oneida* nearly right ahead a couple of miles off, ported her helm in obedience to the law. The *Oneida* not seeing both coloured lights of the *Bombay*, did not at first port, and in fact afterwards starboarded, wrongly so far as seamanship went, but not illegally. In the result the *Bombay* ran into the starboard quarter of the *Oneida*, and sent her with 112 lives to the bottom. There was no attempt to blame the law; the *Bombay* was universally exonerated, and the *Oneida* universally condemned. The *Osprey* saw, some miles distant, and nearly right ahead, the green light of the *Amazon* 'added to' the

It may also be needless to say that the second ship (Y) is left without law or guidance from the moment she becomes aware of the danger into which her obedience to the law had led her. The green light of X alone, which she at length probably sees, is a confirmatory signal to her to put her helm to starboard and turn back again, but there is no distinct license for this, and however naturally wrong she may be, she is legally right. So that in moments of extreme danger, natural and artificial law must fight it out in the mind of the perplexed victim.

The usual—in fact the only—answer to all this is, that if X had seen the proper signals and had obeyed them, all would have been well; which might be logical, if the retention of the particular law were the matter to be desired, and not necessarily the safety of shipping.

It should be needless also to point out that this conflict of natural and artificial law, in the matter of plain signals, is a weaken-

---

red light; and ported her helm. She then saw the red light subtracted from the green, and continued to port her helm. She was ultimately run into on her port quarter by the *Amazon*, and both she and her opponent sank, with the loss of several lives. The *Amazon* was condemned; the *Osprey* exonerated; hardly any one blamed a law which ordered the *Osprey* to disobey the very plain signals she had received. The *Bywell Castle* in the Thames, having ported a little in consequence of seeing the red light of the *Princess Alice* nearly ahead, saw green added to red, gave more port helm in accordance with this law, ran into the starboard side of the *Princess Alice*, sank her, and destroyed 600 lives. The law which counselled port helm for *Bywell Castle*, in direct opposition to the signals she received, was not blamed. The *Bywell Castle* was not blamed. The blame all rested on the shoulders of the *Princess Alice*, though there was not a tittle of evidence to show that she had ever had a signal to do other than she did.

The *Demetrius* saw both side-lights of the *Trojan* nearly right ahead, and ported her helm. She saw the red light disappear and the green light come into view, and she thereupon put her helm hard-a-port, and ran into the starboard side of the *Trojan*. The authoritative journal commenting on the accident, attacks the *Trojan* for making such signals (by her movements), but has no condemnation for the *Demetrius* for disobeying them, nor for the law which counselled her to do so.

The *Northumberland* saw both side-lights of the *Leopard* ahead two miles distant, and ported her helm in obedience to the law. She saw red subtracted from green, and put her helm hard-a-port: she was presently run into on her port side by the *Leopard*. The *Leopard* was condemned; but not the law for counselling the *Northumberland* to disobey a clear signal.

I might go on multiplying cases, but it is needless. The point is clear enough that the action of the law is such as to justify disobedience to plain signals whenever it is done by porting the helm.

ing of the signals all along the line. When the law infers that it is right for a ship to port her helm when green is added to red ahead of her, and she has thereby had a distinct signal *not* to do it, it becomes easy to infer that it is not wrong to starboard the helm when red is added to green in cases not 'end-on, or nearly end-on.' And then we pass on to infer that, after all, the whole of the signals made by these red and green lights are not at all certain, and need not be too much believed in. It is as if the State stepped in with a general law which threw doubts into the mind of every engine-driver as to whether the red light *really* meant an order to pull the train up.

If there were any real want of a law such as Article 15 its demonstrated and too sadly exemplified dangers might be faced. But it is not necessary. The principle was adopted in 1840, when there were no coloured lights, and consequently no such natural and admirable signals as I have described, and it should have disappeared on their advent.* Those who uphold it must declare that a special law is necessary to govern 6° or 7° at the most, of the 360° which bound a ship's horizon, under conditions which must be exceptional, and cannot possibly be permanent.

But it must be noted also, that this Article 15 was drawn in 1860, when there was no other law for steamers invented, and when it was intended that steamers were to depend for their safety on the natural signals made by the red and green lights, and *mutually* avoid one another, except in these 'end-on, or nearly end-on' cases.† Article 16 was not thought of when Article 15 was drawn, and in fact was proposed by France when England thought the rules of the road were complete without it. Had Article 16 been invented first, it is difficult to suppose that Article 15 would ever have seen the light. Article 16 might give the steamer, which has the other to the left of her, the right of way clearly enough. There was, therefore, quite pressure enough in the rare and exceptional case of ships steering exactly the one for the other, with the consequence

* So, practically, said the Judge of the Admiralty Court in 1857.—See Parliamentary Paper, May 17th, 1871, p. 8.

† "A, seeing the green light of B, should starboard; seeing the red light of B, should port," said Dr. Lushington,—*Ibid.*, p. 7.

that *neither* had the right of way, to make one of them—which was all that was necessary—claim the right of way, by altering course to the right (to starboard), not by law, of which we have seen the evil, but by choice, which could be naturally altered, if necessary, without any conflict of law.*

But Article 16, which, properly drawn, would be full of safety to shipping, and still involves sound principles, is so drawn as to be full of dangers and pit-falls. It appears at first sight to be a complete law as it stands, but it is not so, as it only gives directions to one ship of an approaching pair, while the other ship is given different directions in another Article. This is Article 22, and it orders the other ship—which is mentioned but not directed in Article 16—to 'keep her course.' There is a third Article which must be read with, and forms a part of, these two others. This is Article 18, which most probably orders that *both* these ships on approaching are to 'slacken their speed.'

'Crossing,' with 'risk of collision,' clearly means that both ships are steering towards one point, and that the two paths cross one another at this point at larger or smaller angles. That is to say, these three rules, Articles 16, 22, and 18, govern the enormous majority of the conditions under which steam-ships can possibly meet at sea.

If we turn to Article 14 we shall see that the law for two steamers 'crossing' is identical with that for two sailing ships approaching, close-hauled, on opposite tacks; and it is fair to infer that the relative positions sought to be dealt with in the one case, are similar to those sought to be dealt with in the other. The paths of steamers 'crossing,' with 'risk of collision,' may cross at all angles, but those of close-hauled ships must cross at a fixed angle of about 45°, enabling us to construct a diagram exactly representing the circumstances to which Article 14, par. *b*, is

* The dangers of this Article 16 might almost be made to disappear, even if the printed rule remained, were the coloured lights always fitted, and known to be fitted, in strict accordance with Article 3 (*d*), and if the green light did not show on the port bow, nor the red light on the starboard bow, then both lights would never be seen together, and Article 15 at night would lapse. But the Surveyors of the Board of Trade (see 'Instructions to Surveyors,' pp. 78—82) are enjoined to see that the lights show to some indefinite extent on the wrong bow.

intended to apply, and by consequence representing one case of the position of steamers when Article 16 is intended to apply.

Such a diagram is provided in Fig. 3, where X, somewhere on the line A O, is steering towards B; and Y, somewhere on the line C O, is steering towards D, both therefore steering towards O; X might evidently be nearer to O than Y, or Y might be nearer to O than X. X might be going faster than Y, but being further from O, might be nearly equally near in time to O with Y, or *vice versâ*. The exceptional case would evidently be when X and Y were at the same speed, and equally distant from O.

The crossing angle, D O A, is here 45°. With sailing ships close-hauled it could not be materially larger, but it might, if either or both ships were not close-hauled, be diminished to nothing, and then increased again as the ships steered more and more away from the wind.

If we consider this diagram we shall note that the danger of collision is at the point O, and that the only necessity for law to step in is to arrange, by some plain rule, which ship should reach that point first. Any dispute as to which ship had the right to pass first, might lead to a mutual struggle for precedence, and end in collision. It is obvious that the law ought to call upon one of the two ships to yield the right of way to the other, and to let her pass the dangerous point first.

From a date measured almost by hundreds of years up to 1854, British ships, as well as those of all other nations, had a well understood rule that the ship on the port tack—that is, the ship X in Fig. 3—was to yield the right of way. The rule was formulated in different words at different times, but was always clear. Thus it ran:—

"The ship on the starboard tack (Y) is to keep her wind, while that on the larboard tack (X) is always to pass to leeward."—"All ships on the larboard tack are to bear up for those on the starboard tack when passing on opposite tacks."—"When ships are on different tacks, and unavoidably cross near each other, the ship on the starboard tack (Y) is to keep the wind, and that on the larboard tack (X) is always to pass to leeward, except in cases where extreme danger might arise from a strict compliance with this instruction."

—"When both are going by the wind, the vessel on the starboard tack (Y) shall keep her wind, and the one on the larboard tack (X) bear up—thereby passing each other on the larboard hand."—"The ship on the larboard tack (X) shall give way to the ship on the starboard tack (Y)," &c.

Equally confirmatory and clear were the glosses or decisions of the Courts. "A vessel close-hauled on the port-tack ought *never* to put her helm a-lee." In reference to the meaning of the phrase 'give way,' it was settled in the Admiralty Court by the Trinity Master, in the case of the *Mary Rose*, "that a ship ordered to 'give way,' was to "keep out of the way by avoiding the bows and *going astern* of the" other vessel.

That is to say, that in Fig. 3 it was compulsory on X (if it was necessary to make any change whatever) to turn to the right so as to pass behind Y; and she was absolutely forbidden to make any movement tending to claim a right to pass in front of Y. This rule was carried out in principle before the days of steamers in all cases. Of every pair of ships approaching each other, one was always under a law compelling her to let the other pass in front of her. "If she took any other course," said the law courts, "she did it at her own risk." In no case was she justified in not making an attempt to avoid passing in front of the other ship, except in that of extreme danger arising from it.

The wisdom of such a law is obvious from an inspection of Fig. 3. Y, having admittedly the right to continue undisturbed her path towards D, a very slight alteration of course to the right by X will remove all danger of collision; and this because, by turning to the right, X moves the point at which the paths cross, nearer and nearer to Y, and consequently hastens the time at which Y will pass it. If Y is going very much faster than X, the period of danger is by so much shortened; yet no more danger to X arises whether Y be going faster or slower. Y's speed is not an element of danger. But if X were to turn to the left, under starboard helm—supposing she had ability to do so—though she might shorten the time of her own crossing the path of Y, she could have no guarantee of safety, because that would depend on the speed of

Y.* It might easily happen that from Y's nearness to O, or her greater speed, X—if she did not alter her course—could not possibly reach the point O until Y had passed it. In such a case, if X were to turn to the left, she might bring about a collision otherwise impossible.

It is difficult to believe, but it appears to be nevertheless true, that all the clearness of the law which has been described, was deliberately, and with purpose, destroyed by the framers of the law of 1863, which is that still in force for these close-hauled vessels. The words 'give way,' 'bear up,' 'pass to leeward,' 'pass astern,' &c., were deliberately rejected in favour of the words 'keep out of the way,' and so far as can now be ascertained, with the view of giving to X the option of making a movement to pass in front of Y, if she thought she could effect that object.

Presumably, the view was that there might be cases where it was not practicable for X to pass astern of Y. Nothing but close proximity, and therefore 'immediate danger,' could bring about such a state of things; the cases—if there were such—were clearly exceptional, and were intended to be fully provided for under the present Article 23, which descends from 1863, and at any rate professed to guard against a blind obedience to a law, under conditions which made it dangerous.

It will be perceived that though I am dealing up to this point with the case of ships 'close-hauled on opposite tacks,' I am illustrating a principle, and I shall presently show that this principle is of general application.

But before passing from this particular case, I must note that at night, the only signal X can get, warning him to put the law in force, is the appearance of a red light somewhere in the direction X, Z. He cannot depend on any estimate of its distance; but if he watches it carefully, he can detect, after some lapse of time, whether its direction is altering or not. If it is not altering, he is warned that the danger is great and growing, and that on him lies the onus of avoiding it.

* It is proper to note that the paths drawn for the ships in these diagrams when turning are those of a ship neither the best nor the worst manœuvrer of the many tried.

Under the old law—had red and green side-lights been in use—such a signal would have been as absolute and precise in its meaning as the red light on a railway. Under the new law it tells him he must 'keep out of the way,' and that he is as likely to do so by turning to the left as by turning to the right, though, as we have seen, the turn to the right is nearly certain to be absolutely safe, while the turn to the left is nearly as certain to lead to danger.*

Passing now to the more general principles, it is to be noted that statistics show that the vast majority of all the collisions which occur between ships under way, whatever their classes may be, are preceded by an approach similar to that shown in Fig. 3. The angle D O A, at which the courses cross, is rarely greater than 45°, and generally less. The signals made by the lights are very often as clear as those which have been described, and the enormous majority of such collisions take place when one of the two ships has either neglected to make any movement to pass astern of the other, or has made some movement to endeavour to pass in front of her.

If we consider X and Y in Fig. 3 as steamers, the law is just as we have seen it for sailing vessels. X can get no other signal at night than the steamer's red light of Y, and its change, or no

* That I may not be said to err or exaggerate, I will quote Vice-Admiral De Horsey's directions to X, being a ship close hauled on the port tack, how to obey the law, on seeing Y.

1st. Take bearing.

2nd. Ascertain whether a steamer or not.

3rd. If a steamer, keep your course.

4th. If a sailing vessel—

(*a*) If to windward of you, keep your course.

(*b*) If ahead of you, or less than two or three points on lee bow, keep your course.

(*c*) If to leeward of you, or more than two or three points on lee bow—

1. Take bearing again.

2. If her bearing has altered materially, and continues to alter, keep your course.

3. If her bearing has not altered materially, *tack, or bear away* until it does so.—'The Rule of the Road at Sea,' by Vice-Admiral De Horsey, 1883.

So also was the Wreck Commissioners' dictum in the case of the *Avalanche* (where two ships were destroyed). "The *Avalanche* (X) had the option either of going ahead or astern of the *Forest* (Y) as she thought fit."

It must be noted that Admiral De Horsey writes not as to what ought to be, but as rigidly adhering to what the law says.

change, of direction. Under such conditions, the old law, had it been applied, would have directed that "the steamer which had the other on her own starboard side, should turn to the right and pass astern of the other." And the courts and other authorities in their glosses, would have said that X—the steamer ordered to yield the right of way—"must *never* put her helm a-starboard to turn to the left."

True, there might be cases of close proximity where X had no room to turn so as to pass astern, but such cases, being those of 'immediate danger,' would have been considered as duly provided for in Article 23, and would not have come under the law at all.

The new law is, however, drawn so that this Article 23 has no relation whatever to X. She is directed only to "keep out of the way" of Y, and the authoritative explanation of this phrase, "keep out of the way," is, "X must get out of the way by stopping, or *going ahead, or starboarding,* or porting, or going astern, as the circumstances of the case may require." *

We are thus met by an absolute conflict between the principle of the old law and that of the new.† We have seen that of the old law to be the settlement of the only question arising, namely, which of the two ships was to let the other pass in front of her. The new law leaves this just as unsettled as if there were no law, and calls on the mariner in X, Fig. 3, to decide that point for himself, on the spur of the moment.

But now we must observe that while X is left absolutely free to make every possible movement (if Article 18 should not be intended to be binding on him, as by the authoritative gloss just quoted, it might not be), and therefore cannot 'depart,' under Article 23, from any rule; Y is, by Article 22, bound not to deviate from her course until danger becomes immediate, or as it has been naïvely said, "until it appears to be too late." ‡

Under the old law something to this effect was certainly said in

* 'Regulations for preventing Collisions at Sea. By authority,' 1869.

† That is, between the law of crossing ships before 1854, and since 1863.

‡ 'Rule of the Road,' by Thomas Gray, 1878, p. 38, quoted in next chapter.

bygone days, as I have already quoted; and it was more reasonable to say it, when the order was that X was on no account to attempt to cross that course.

Thus, had red and green lights been in use under the old laws, Y would have been more reasonably ordered not to deviate from her course on seeing the green light of X approaching, because she had a right to expect to see presently, the red light 'added to the green,' which would assure her of safety.

But when it is made lawful for X to try and cross in front of Y, Y has no right to expect any safety signal, and is asked to stand on helplessly into the growing danger which is announced to her by the continuance in view of X's green light only.

Every now and then we read of the most painful cases of mariners in this position. Bound not to alter their ship's course, as far as the law can bind them, and yet conscious that the danger is becoming more imminent, they try many futile methods of altering the state of affairs. Too often they lose their heads in the puzzle, and do what is absolutely the very worst thing they could do, and we hear of it in the report of the ultimate collision.

If X in Fig. 3, and in all similar cases, is free—as she undoubtedly is by the law—to try to pass in front of Y, Y ought equally to be free to escape the danger of the movement. "Seeing green," in the words of the late judge of the Admiralty Court, she ought to be free to 'starboard' her helm, so as to yield X the right of way which she herself had been deprived of.

Again, the slackening of speed under Article 18, if it is, as it certainly was, binding on both ships approaching, like X and Y, is demonstrably dangerous when combined with Article 16.* If X were bound not to try to cross the path of Y, as she would have

* It is necessary to qualify any belief as to the binding action of Article 18, in consequence of the change of phrase introduced into the last issue of 'Steering and Sailing Rules.' Article 18 was formerly Article 16, and ran: "Every steam-ship, when approaching another ship, so as to involve risk of collision, shall slacken her speed, or, if necessary, stop and reverse. . . ." It was as if the slacking of speed was binding, whether thought necessary or not, while the stopping and reversing was at discretion. The new phrase: "shall slacken her speed, or stop and reverse, if necessary," would rather appear to make the whole thing discretionary. But then if this was intended, the shorter way would have been to have omitted the Article altogether, as there is no law left in it.

been under the old law, every reduction of speed she made could only assist her, and make assurance doubly sure. If Y adopts reduction of speed as a measure of precaution until she gets the safety signal of the red light of X, the act cannot, except in cases of close proximity, hinder the action of X in trying to pass astern. But if X, determining to exercise her option in trying to pass in front of Y, should feel herself bound by Article 18 to reduce her speed, she is doing all that it is possible for her to do to make collision certain. If she determines to try to pass in front of Y, her only chance of safety lies in high speed, so as to make sure of passing the crossing point before Y can reach it; every second's delay is a second added to the danger, and to reduce speed is to delay. It is a common precursor of collision for X to turn to the left in her endeavour to 'get out of the way' of Y, and to reduce her speed at the same time. The combination is perfectly legal, and perfectly fatal also.*

At sea, at night, the vast majority of red or green lights which come into view, are seen a little on one bow, right ahead, or a little on the other bow. This is a condition following on the circumstances of sea traffic. They are admirable signals, almost perfect, when properly fitted, and of full power. The green light to the right, or the red light to the left, are nearly always announcements of safety, while the green light to the left, or the red light to the right, are always danger signals. Naturally, and apart from law, a green light to the left is always a signal to alter course to the

* The following are illustrations, taken from a series of Maritime Dispositions, published in the 'Shipping Gazette':

The *Arabian* ports, stops, and reverses, to a green light on port bow, and runs into the starboard side of the *Colorado*.

The *Grebe* sees a red light on the starboard bow, puts helm hard a-starboard, stops, and reverses, and runs into the port bow of the *Dagmar*.

The *Braganza* starboards, stops, and reverses to a red light on the starboard bow, and runs into the port side of the *Pera*, and sinks her.

The *Alexandra* ports, eases, and stops, to a vessel (which presently shows a green light) on the port bow. The vessel all but clears her in passing ahead of her.

The *Talbot* ports, stops, and reverses to a green light on the port bow, and is run into on the port bow by the *Blink Bonnie*.

The *Demetrius* ports, stops, and reverses to red subtracted from green, three points on her port bow, and runs into the starboard side of the *Trojan*.

The *Countess of Galloway* ports, to a green light a little on her port bow, then eases and stops, and is run into on the port side by the *Hipparchus*, &c.

left (*i.e.* to starboard the helm); while the red light to the right is always a signal to alter course to the right (*i.e.* to port the helm), and this natural law was approved by the Judge of the Admiralty Court in 1857. If the principles of the old law for close-hauled ships were in force for all classes of ships alike, then a green light to the left would always call for caution, and watching for the addition of the red light as the safety signal; while the red light to the right would retain its natural significance, and *always* call on the ships seeing it, to turn to the right, except where some other circumstance showed it dangerous to do so.

But owing to the loss of the old principles in the new laws, and to the glosses—some of which I have quoted—which have followed, there is no agreement amongst seamen as to what the lights really mean, and Vice-Admiral De Horsey, when he comes to draw up 'practical rules' in accordance with the law, finds it necessary almost entirely to ignore the use of the coloured lights, and to teach the mariner to act without their aid.

I have dealt in preceding pages with cases where the ships are so far apart that their manœuvring powers do not come into question, that is, where there is no doubt about the law. If the rules are examined as to their action when the distances are small enough to involve questions of manœuvring powers, all the considerations already put forward are doubly enforced.

As an illustration, I may take a very common condition of crossing between two ships set forth in Fig. 4. As before, the paths I have shown for two ships in turning are those for a ship, not the best and yet not the worst of those measured and mapped out. They are quite reliable, as they are the mean of three turns, none of which differ by more than a few feet in distances measured by between one and two thousand. X and Y are supposed to be steamers approaching under conditions similar to those in Fig. 3, but only about half the distance apart (about 500 yards if the ships were 325 feet long). It is to be supposed that thick weather has so obscured the lights that they have not been seen till now.

Beside the shortening of the distance apart, the only other differences made are the slight enlargement of the 'crossing angle,' and placing X nearer the crossing point than Y is. In Fig. 3, Y was rather the nearer of the two.

The manœuvring powers allowed to each of these ships are equal. They represent a case, which has been most carefully measured, of a ship with steam steering gear, large rudder, and large helm angle. The powers of turning developed are rather below the average of good manœuvring ships, but may not impossibly represent better turning powers than are generally seen in the mercantile marine. It must be understood that in single screw ships the turns exhibited cannot be improved except perhaps slightly by a skilful reversal of the engines at the proper time. But even in this case the difference it is possible to effect in the first 4 points (45° and 13 intervals of time—65 seconds at 12 knots) is very slight. Greater or less original speed, it is to be observed, does not in general materially affect the space required by a ship to turn in. The lines in the diagram show approximately the varying positions of the line of keel of the ships in process of turning; and the figures show where her bow would be at the end of each interval of time. The small circles on the straight lines with numbers against them, show, in like manner, where the ship's bow would be at the end of each interval of time, had she continued her course.

The first glance at the figure shows us that though the ships are some 500 yards apart, and approaching quite in the ordinary way, it is a physical impossibility, so far as space is concerned, for X, a steamer "having another on her own starboard side" to "keep out of the way" of that steamer, if she, Y, "keeps her course." No matter what X does with her helm, she cannot avoid the crossing point, and if Y, by keeping her course, happens to be near the spot when X reaches it, collision ensues.

On the other hand, Y can quite easily avoid the crossing point entirely. And the figure shows that if she puts her helm hard a-starboard, she not only avoids collision, but makes it impossible. It is just as impossible for X to strike Y, if Y puts her helm hard a-starboard, as it is for X to avoid the crossing point, by any use of her helm.

Let us pause for a moment to see what natural law—coloured

lights being in use, and properly fitted—has to say to a case of this kind. We have considered it to arise from thick weather, but the ships might easily have seen each other a minute before, and half a mile apart, and have got into the condition shown, merely while pausing to observe whether the bearings of the lights were altering. But on discovering either the lights apparently rather close, or having watched for a time and observed the danger denoted by no change of bearing, natural law would dictate port helm and reduced speed to X; and starboard helm and reduced speed to Y; because X would be obeying the natural signal of a *red* light to her right; and Y would be obeying the natural signal of a *green* light to her left.

We can see at once the exceptional case where obedience to such natural signals would be dangerous. If the curve that X describes in turning towards Y were to coincide with that which Y describes in turning towards X, and each ship were to persevere—no doubt there would be collision. But this could only happen when the courses crossed at *one* particular point, equally distant from each ship, and the manœuvring powers of the ships were equal. In the figure, the nearer the crossing point was to X, when Y's distance from it remained unchanged, so much the more certain to avoid collision is Y's starboard helm. Then, as the crossing point is moved away from X towards the 7th interval of time, so does the danger of this obedience to the natural law grow—but then so also does the distance apart of the ships grow, and consequently time to avoid mistakes. But the moment the point of greatest danger is past, safety in obedience to natural signals begins again.

There is no difficulty on these simple and unassailable grounds in condemning any stress which is laid upon Y to "keep her course" rather than to yield and starboard her helm, if she has the slightest shadow of doubt. So must Article 22 of the rules be strongly deprecated as dangerous in its inception; more strongly must those glosses be condemned which tend to add to, rather than to diminish, the force of the law.

It is one thing—using Fig. 4 in illustration—to forbid Y, being the holding-on ship, to port her helm and turn to the right, across the bows of X; and quite another thing to forbid her to move in a greater or less degree, for the stern of X. In the first case, she can rarely by such a movement help X to avoid the crossing point, but may often make a collision, not otherwise possible. As in the case before us, if the speeds were equal, the stern of X would just have passed the danger point before the bow of Y reached it, but ever so little port helm by Y would make collision certain. Yet starboard helm by Y can hardly make a collision not otherwise almost inevitable, unless the changes in the light signals are disobeyed. If we look at the changing directions in the lines of keel in these ships while turning, we can see that while Y could not get any change of signal at all, no matter what X did, X must get a *green* light—or safety signal—in very little over three intervals of Y's time. Of course X has no business to keep port helm after this, and the mere righting of the helm would save a collision in such cases at very much closer quarters than those represented here.

I have not yet much considered the effect of differences of speed in this case; before doing so, it might be well to point out that it is exceedingly unlikely that X should have any idea of her inability to avoid a collision with Y. A *red* light as much as 3 points on the starboard bow, would seldom be held to be an immediate danger. It would no doubt be recognized as one if it seemed to approach without materially changing its bearing. But even then, inevitable collision with a red light 500 yards off and 3 points on the starboard bow would not be looked for, I venture to say, by any officer in a steamer (say) 320 feet long going at moderate speed. Yet the conditions here are that, unless Y takes the duty of avoiding it, collision is absolutely certain, if the speed of Y should be in a very small degree superior to that of X.

Nor would Y, under the present state of the law, regard herself as having any special warning *not* to keep her course. It is a serious thing to disobey the clear law, when there are no glosses to help you, but many to force obedience almost at all risks. And a green light a point and a half on the bow, 500 yards off, would seldom be considered to justify "a departure from the rules." The law embodied in Article 22 in fact has been drawn in absence of clear comprehension of what it leads to. Under the impression that it has prescribed a measure generally safe, it has ordered one generally dangerous, which ought, if established at all, to be fenced about with great cautions. It has been thought that there was, in the general case, more danger—especially at night—in a mutual turn towards each other of two approaching ships, than of the rigid keeping of her course by one. The fact is not so. The mutual turn of two ships towards one another, will—speaking of the general case—be either undertaken at distances when safety signals are made to prevent its being carried too far; * or else, at shorter distances, when it becomes the only possible way of avoiding a collision. Recurring for a moment to the question of relative speed, or the increase and reduction thereof, it may be recalled that the figure 4 is so drawn as to intervals of time, that if they were equal for both ships, X would be just across the bow of Y when the latter reached the crossing point, supposing each ship continued her course and speed. Were X a very little slower than Y, there would be collision at the crossing point of their courses. Now if the relative speeds were such as to make a collision at the crossing point, it is evident that equal decreases, or equal increases, would not mend matters in the least. Secondly, if collision is to be avoided by differences of speed alone, there should be increase to X and decrease to Y. If the law infers anything whatever on this head, it rather infers the decrease to X, as she is the ship which by some alteration of condition is to "keep out of the way" of Y, presuming that Y will keep her course. There can be little to show X that she wants an increase rather than a decrease, and Article 18, if it presses anything on her, presses a decrease of speed; that is, so far, presses a dangerous act on her. The act is not dangerous in the general case, nor is it in this case—it is neutral—if Y has license to starboard her helm. The safety signal which follows this act of Y, cancels any order X may have had to reduce her speed. Y, by reason of her greater distance from the crossing point, has *primâ facie* the greatest facilities for reducing speed. And, while Y, by reducing speed, may benefit X if the course is not altered, it cannot possibly make matters worse if Y starboards her helm to the *green*

* There is a very small proportion of such collisions, but then there is always disobedience to the signals made by the lights.

light. There is but one case in which Y can be wrong in reducing her speed, that is, if she ports her helm, and turns to the right. She is then making the combined movement which, of all others, is most likely to produce collision. She is endeavouring to cross in front of X, before X can come up to the crossing-point, and she is delaying the time when she herself will reach the crossing-point.*

It has been necessary to pause, and examine the case illustrated in this diagram at some length, because its general conditions are the usual precursors of collisions. But either ships never turn towards one another as shown for X and Y, or else they always avoid collision when they do so; for there are practically no collisions preceded by these movements. On the other hand, collisions used to be most frequent (38 per cent.) when X ported and Y ported; that is, when each turned to his own right, under the influence of the old port helm rule. They were next, and probably now are, most frequent (24 per cent.), when X turns to the left, and Y turns to the right. The next stage of frequency (21 per cent.) was when Y kept her course, and X turned to the left. The least frequent but two (11 per cent.), was when Y kept her course, and X turned to the right. In all these cases (94 per cent.) if lights are seen, the natural signals would be disobeyed either actively or passively, and in too many cases, not illegally.

Almost the least frequent of all (a little more than 2 per cent.) are these cases of each ship turning towards the other; but then there was always disobedience to the safety signal. The least frequent of all were—probably—the inevitable accidents when neither ship took any steps whatever.

To summarize briefly what has been said in the preceding pages, I may put it that:—

(1) There is an admirable system of coloured lights established

* The transparent diagrams, when applied to each other, will show that when there is the least difference between the two ships, the *outer ship* in a mutual turn of two towards each other, will always get the safety signal of the change of colour of light at night, which will enable her to right her helm with confidence. Only in the case when the two ships are in all respects equal, and turning opposite ways *on the same arc*, does this great element of safety fail.

afloat, capable of giving distinct signals leading to the safety of ships in view of them.

(2) These are really *helm signals*, telling the mariner (if not interfered with by law or gloss):—

THAT IN ALL CASES—

Red is a signal not to turn *to the left.*
Green is a signal not to turn *to the right.*

THAT IN CASES OF DOUBT OR ALARM IN THE ABSENCE OF OTHER INDICATIONS—

Red is a signal to turn *to the right.*
Green is a signal to turn *to the left.*

(3) But the mistaken law, and the more mistaken glosses, have stepped in to an extent which has entirely confused these plain signals, and left ships almost as free to disobey as to obey them.

(4) Much of the confusion has arisen from not clearly understanding the principles of the old Rule of the Road, and from mixing up the proper domain of any 'Rule of the Road' with that limited domain where there is 'immediate danger.' A Rule of the Road presupposes time and space enough to carry it out in, which is admitted by the introduction of Article 23, providing that where there may not be such time and space, the rule must not be too rigidly adhered to should it seem to be dangerous.

(5) At the same time, I have critically examined, I think, all the positions, and the chief of the varied conditions, under which ships at sea can possibly meet, and am able to say that it is only in a small minority of cases where obedience to the signals made by the lights does not tend to remove the chance of collision.* I am also able to say that movements in disobedience to the signals made by the lights are nearly always present in cases of collision.

(6) Similar language may be held relative to collisions in clear daylight and in fog. Movements in themselves dangerous, but not clearly condemned by law or practice, are nearly always present before collision.

* Chapter III. shows how the inquirer can make these examinations for himself.

The remedies for the state of things remarked on are simple enough. Let the law settle which of any two ships steering for the same point, is to have the right to pass in front of the other, and forbid the other to make any movement which shall tend to refuse that right. Secondly, let it be laid down that in any cases where it shall appear to the ship having this right of way, that it will be dangerous to assert it, she is to abandon her claim, and manœuvre to pass astern of the other.

In a word, return to the principles of law which governed sea traffic from ancient times till 1854, and were lost in 1863.

At night, such laws would call on the 'giving way ship'—to use the old term—in all cases to obey the signals made by the coloured lights; and would call on the 'holding-on ship' to obey the signals made by the lights in every case where it appeared to be in the slightest degree dangerous to keep her course.

My own opinion is that there should be one simple rule for all classes of ships; and being pressed to do so, I formulated such a rule for the Thames Traffic Committee in these words:—

"No ship shall have the right to cross the bow of any other ship from port to starboard." * If the distinction between steamers and sailing vessels were to be maintained, the words 'under steam' would require to be inserted after 'ship.'

What we require is a rule which shall plainly settle which of the two ships has the right to pass on, and yet at the same time to avoid investing this right with anything like compulsion in its exercise. The negative form adopted above seems to me the best for this purpose, but if some positive element is required in the rule—which I rather doubt—a law for steamers alone might run thus, without infringing on any of the principles enunciated:

"A ship under steam may cross the bows of another, leaving her on the port hand; but no ship under steam has the right to cross the bows of another, leaving her on the starboard hand."

I am sure that the more such a rule as either of these is examined, the more its comprehensiveness, simplicity, and safety, will shine out.

* Report, Thames Traffic Committee, p. 471.

CHAPTER II.

THE TEACHING RELATIVE TO THE 'RULE OF THE ROAD,' CURRENT IN THE MERCANTILE MARINE.*

THIS book is in many ways remarkable. In one way, from the authoritative style of the author, writing for seamen on a highly technical subject, of which he cannot possibly have any of that knowledge which would properly allow of an authoritative style. Again, as to style, from the mixture of the deprecatory with the authoritative, and side by side with it. Then in the denial that the author is proposing rules of seamanship, when every page bristles with them.

Thus in the Introduction (p. 26, ed. 1878), he writes:—"Apprentices and others who are desirous of getting on would do well to master these lessons, so as to be able to answer every question in the beginning of the book. Examiners and teachers will find them useful as aids to their work, while masters and officers will, I trust, not take them amiss; and by the kindly help of the practised master they may bear good fruit." These words show the authoritative and deprecatory styles side by side. The succeeding language appears to be entirely deprecatory, but is far indeed from properly describing the contents of the preceding pages.

"What is written in them is not a guide to seamanship. How to handle a ship so as to keep out of the way of another is a

* 'Observations on the "Rule of the Road" at Sea; prepared for, and dedicated to, Officers and Seamen of the Mercantile Marine;' by Thomas Gray (Assistant-Secretary Marine Department Board of Trade). (4th Edition and 10th Thousand.) London: Pewtress and Co., 1884. 2nd Thousand, 1878.

matter for the sailor, only to be learnt by observation, experience, and practice; it is the business of his practical life. These pages merely set out the rules, the official regulations, and the law, so far as they refer to the sort of lights a ship is to carry, how they are to be fitted, what signals a sailor may make, and how and when he may make them; which of two ships drawing dangerously near to each other is required by law to keep on her course, and which to keep out of the way. They also especially show the cases in which the rules do not apply, and distinguish them from cases in which the rules do apply; in short, they show what the rules require, and leave the question "how to do it?" to be settled by experience, and by the sixth and greatest of all senses—common sense."

Now, if we turn to the questions at the beginning of the book (pp. 8 and 9)* which "apprentices and others" are to find answered therein, and which answers will be useful to "examiners and teachers," we discover such as the following:—

"Should I alter my ship's course at once, on seeing the side-light of another ship, or should I wait a little and watch?"

"If I think the giving way ship does not see me, what should I do, and why?"

"If two steamers are crossing at this angle , how can the position be most readily converted into one of safety, and by which ship?"

"State the danger of porting to a *green* light seen ahead or anywhere on the port bow, or of starboarding to a *red* light seen ahead or anywhere on the starboard bow?"

"In approaching another steamer with danger of collision, and with no room or time for getting out of the way, or altering my course by turning my ship's head, what am I to do?"

All these questions are evidently just what is denied of them. The answers to them must be "guides to seamanship" and directions "how to handle a ship." As if to make this plain, the author has headed his questions with the statement that "it would be well if officers placed in charge of a watch could answer" them.†

* At the end of the Book in ed. 1884.

† In one place the author goes so far as to prescribe the sail which a ship shall carry, p. 36, ed. 1884.

Possibly as remarkable as the foregoing, is the strange way in which directly opposing statements and teachings are brought into juxtaposition throughout the book, and the elaborate methods adopted for explaining the obvious.*

It is sometimes as if the author were puzzling out on paper the *pros* and *cons* of some difficult problem of which he had in no way approached the solution.

Of the side by side contrarieties we have a prominent and highly dangerous example in the very first page of the first section of what forms the body of the book—the "Statement and explanation of the statutes and the rules." The section is headed "The Ship's Lights," and begins thus:—

"I must see that the *red* and *green* side-lights which my ship, in common with all other sea-going ships, is to carry, are powerful enough to show for two miles on a dark clear night; that they are fitted within board screens reaching at least three (3) feet forward from the lamps; *that they cannot be seen across the bows.*"

Four lines lower down we have:—"As I know that the rays of the side-lights *must in every ship cross at some distance ahead,* I ought to find out what that distance is in my ship, so that I may know *how far on each of my bows a ship nearly ahead of me, will see both of my side-lights.*"

The first statement is correct and the second utterly wrong. The rays of the *green* light must not by law, and need not in practice, cross to the port bow, and the rays of the *red* light must not by law, and need not in practice, cross to the starboard bow. The correct and the incorrect directions as to the fitting of the side-lights stand side by side, without a word of explanation, and are emphasized by a diagram making each light visible quite ten degrees on the wrong bow.

While there is thus no distinction drawn between 'yes' and 'no' in matters where a precise distinction is absolutely necessary to ordinary safety of sea traffic, there are statements which are in

* The most striking instance of the latter is the following:—"The rule just quoted, which says that 'a ship *shall* go at a moderate speed,' does not mean that every ship shall, as soon as a fog comes on, get under way . . . . If at anchor, when a fog comes on, she may remain at anchor . . . ." Ed. 1878, p. 17.

every way to be commended, scattered through the book with as much apparent unconsciousness of their firm truth as there is of the other statements' fallacy.

The curious way in which the 'Rules of the Road,' which, if they are to be of any use, should be simple and brief, are expanded over some 90 pages of print and illustration, reads like a strong condemnation of the rules themselves, or else seems labour rather misapplied.

Perhaps the best way to criticise the nature of the teaching spread in ten thousand directions, will be to turn to some of the questions, and then to look up the answers to them. With this view I will take a question on section 3 (ed. 1884) headed, "Dangers of Reckless Port Helm."

"In what case, and in what case only, am I required by the regulations to alter the course of my ship's head to starboard, or, in other words, to 'port my helm?'

The answer is found in rhyme at page 42, and in prose at page 22. The rhyme says:—

"When all three lights I see ahead,
I port my helm, and show my *red*."

The prose answer runs thus:—

"In the present rules there is one case, and only one case, in which I am ordered by law to port my helm. I must recollect this; and recollect that it is a special case, and that when I am required by law to port, the vessel meeting me is also required by law to port. It is not one of two ships only, but both of the two ships that are required by law to port in this case, and that is (at night) when I can see both of the other's side-lights, and the other ship can see both of mine."

Now, either these poetical and prose directions are intended to be mere paraphrases of the law; or else they are glosses or directions as to how the law is to be interpreted and acted upon. In either case, let it be remembered that the author is dealing with lights which he considers should show 10° on the wrong bow, and let my remarks on Article 15 at page 15 *et seq.*, be also borne in mind, and the danger of such paraphrases or glosses may be easily seen.

The writer gives no word of warning as to the palpable dangers set out by his own words; and shows no consciousness of the constant disputes in collision cases as to what lights were seen, and the many collisions which the 'reckless' porting he recommends have given rise to. But his paraphrases—if they are such —are incorrect. Bad as the rule is, it is not quite so bad as the gloss. The author's gloss says, "Assume that when you see three lights ahead, the officer in the ship showing them, not only sees your three lights, but sees them ahead, and *then act as if you were certain of it.*" The law is—or was—a trifle more cautious. It told you to slacken speed; and it ordered that when steamships were meeting end-on, or nearly end-on, "*with risk of collision,*" the helms of *both* were to be put to port. The law, bad as it is, only thinks of a mutual agreement, and does not press it as our author does, when he practically says, "When I consider I ought to port, the other ship *is ordered* to port."

The true teaching under this law, if it is to be retained, is derived, not from what is evolved from any inner consciousness, however acute, but from what is actually found to happen at sea. The mariner must be told that he has no guarantee that the other ship will port, as he can have no guarantee that she has had the necessary signal to do so. That he must *on no account* port if *green* was added to *red* ahead of him, and that if he ports in obedience to what he considers is the law, he must be prepared instantly to reverse his helm in case—which experience shows to be very likely—the *red* light of the other ship should disappear. Not a word says our author of all this. On the contrary, he rather seems to counsel port helm in all cases of seeing 'three lights ahead,' even should the consequences be collision, for he says, "If I do port in any other case and get into collision, it will be my own fault," the inference being that it cannot be your fault if you port on seeing three lights ahead.

Then immediately follows a perfectly sound piece of seamanship. "I know that if I port my helm to a *green* light ahead, or anywhere nearly ahead, I am very likely to run into it."

This being a perfectly sound dictum, the wonder is whether our author was aware that a man who has ported to three lights ahead at sea, constantly finds himself under the port helm with a *green* light only ahead. And, if he was aware of it, how he managed to avoid adding:—"therefore if when you have ported to three lights ahead, you see *red* disappear, you should instantly reverse your helm if you wish to avoid collision."

Section 4 is headed, 'I see a light,' and the first question put on it is, "When I see a white light alone, what does it denote?—and what should I do?"

And here let it be noted that the author always appears to think that everything at sea relating to collisions is quite as clear as it is on paper. 'Ahead' is not, with him, that rather vague direction which is at night so difficult to limit. 'Close-hauled' is 'close-hauled;' 'free' and 'wind aft' are clearly divided off in his mind, notwithstanding the immense difficulties which every sailing collision case presents of determining the limits which govern these terms. So also a 'green' light is, in his mind, unmistakeable for any other colour; and all other lights as distinctly plain. And this notwithstanding that he has in another part of his book drawn attention to the effect of changes of atmosphere on colour.

So here in this section; far from uttering any cautions as to the liability to error, he not only assumes that no uncertainty hangs about any light, but when pointing out that a single white light gives, under the law, no less than *four* different signals, without anything to show which is which; he hardly stops to make a remark, and certainly utters no adequate caution. "If," he says, "it is the masthead light of a steamer, I can only at first watch it and wait, taking care to get ready to act if necessary when I see one of the coloured side-lights appear." That is to say:—

"Though there is nothing to show me that the white light I see is the masthead light of a steamer, yet I am to know that it is such, and am to expect the confirmation of my knowledge by the only appearance which could give me that knowledge."

The author points out that trawlers often illegally display a misleading single white light. But in effect, it would not appear that to add a fifth to the four diverse meanings of the white light can be more than proportionately dangerous; especially when it is recollected that trawlers at work are, after all, very nearly stationary.

It is perhaps hardly satisfactory to find that in the answer to the question, "What should I do?" under these confessedly dangerous conditions of law and illegality, there is no advice to be given, beyond apparently—waiting and watching. Yet there ought to be sound advice forthcoming somewhat in these terms:—

"It being well known that very frequent collisions occur from assuming a wrong meaning out of the several capable of being signalled by a single white light, the utmost caution must be used, and no assumption made. As the only further indication which can be got out of a white light is its possible change of bearing, it will generally be a sound precaution to bring it right ahead (if any doubts exist). If your ship's head is then kept steady, change of bearing in the light is readily detected, as your own motion does not then affect the apparent motion of the light, and its true motion to the right or left will show whether it is carried by a ship under way, and what helm will be legal or necessary to avoid collision. Never port the helm to a doubtful light seen on the port bow; and never starboard the helm to a doubtful light seen on the starboard bow. These are movements demonstrably dangerous, and they have led to frequent collisions."

Our author goes on:—

"Generally.—On seeing a single *red* or *green* light, I know only that the ship's head is directed within certain (10) points; but I do not know the distance of the light, the course of the ship, nor the speed of the ship. Her distance, direction, and speed are all unknown to me. I must, therefore, be careful not to act in a hurry on seeing a light, but watch it for awhile, so as to be able to act with certainty, and in good time, when I have to act."

There is so curious a mixture of wisdom and something else in these words that were they not distributed among merchant seamen by the thousand, one might be tempted to smile. But I should think their effect must be exceedingly pernicious on the mind of any seaman studying the Rule of the Road.

For the student could only think the whole thing terribly uncertain and dangerous: that a plainly seen *red* light conveys no signal, and that a plainly seen *green* light conveys no signal. Moreover, it will seem that as the *red* or *green* light, when he first sees it, cannot give him the distance, the course (except within wide limits), or the speed of the ship carrying it—therefore it will always remain more or less of an even chance what he ought to do. For if, as seems to be said, distance, course, and speed of the other vessel are necessary to be known before he can act, *he never can act;* for the *green* or the *red* light will *never show* him any of these things. Yet, if the paragraph were not otherwise calculated to set the seaman's wits all abroad, the caution "not to act in a hurry" would be sound advice.

What should the seaman be taught in opposition to the idea that a single coloured light when first plainly made out does not mean anything?

Probably something of this kind—

"GREEN LIGHT.

"(1) If any helm is wanted, it will almost certainly be 'starboard' helm.

"(2) If it is to the left of the 'keel line' there is more or less danger, which 'starboard' helm, if it is legal or necessary, may remove.

"(3) If it is to the right of the 'keel-line,' there is probably no danger.

"RED LIGHT.

"(1) If any helm is wanted, it will almost certainly be 'port' helm.

"(2) If it is to the right of the 'keel-line,' there is more or less danger, which 'port helm,' if it is legal or necessary, may remove.

"(3) If it is to the left of the 'keel-line,' there is probably no danger.*

"EITHER RED OR GREEN.

"Beyond the colour of the light there is no further information

* Our author has elsewhere written—

"Green to green—or red to red
Perfect safety—go ahead!"

—which is hardly correct, except for lights well to the right or left. Green nearly ahead has—experience tells us—a great tendency to change to red. And red nearly ahead has nearly an equal tendency to change to green; while yet on the otherwise safe bow.

to be got except its change, or no change, of bearing. With a danger light (as above) rapid change of bearing means lessening danger. *No change of bearing means growing danger.*"

It must certainly be considered phenomenal that a teacher upholding the law as it stands, and distributing his teaching in ten thousand directions, should prefer to make out that practically' the established coloured lights when first clearly seen give no useful information, rather than to plainly state the very satisfactory truths above set forth. But it is a part of the oddity of the whole book under review that much of what is said above is to be extracted from some of its other pages.

The next section (ed. 1884) is headed, "I see two lights;" and it is first pointed out that two white lights, one over another, denote a steamer towing a ship. It is then correctly stated, that a fishing-boat drifting to her nets or riding at her lines, shows under the later law, in certain directions, two white lights over one another But there is not the sign of a caution, or even of drawing attention to the chances of false signals being thus conveyed. Yet the danger is not to be ignored, for in fishing-grounds the two white lights, one over the other, may be so frequent a signal that the steamer towing may escape notice until close 'on board' of you, and wrong helm may follow in the excitement of the moment. Probably nothing beyond the strong caution can be given as advice, seeing that the lights in a fishing fleet will be so numerous.

Section 6 (ed. 1884), treats of what are generally called the "not under control lights," and the author, as usual, seems to think that three red lights must always appear as three red lights; never as two, never as one. That two red lights with a white light between them will always be as plain a signal at sea as it is in the study, that the white light will never appear alone, to add another false signal to the 4 shown possible with a single white light. Yet there are on record experiments, 30 years old or more, showing the contrary facts; and very precise experiments, the details of which were handed in to a select committee of the House of Commons by the author himself in 1880, confirming the old experiments in the most absolute manner. The difficulty is to understand why the author should have preferred to publish inferences which he must have known were fallacious, rather than to have stated the true facts when he had them officially before him.

Section 8 (ed. 1884) treats of the very important matter of "sound signals in fogs," and one of two very sensible questions asked is, "What should I first do on hearing a sound signal in fog, mist, or falling snow?" and equally to be commended is much of the advice given in answer, though it is mixed with what cannot be approved, and stops short of giving the kernel of the whole matter.

Thus he speaks of one case :—

"*A whistle*. . . . If I am in a steamer. . . . When, in fog, mist, or falling snow, I hear the steam-whistle of another steamer, and the sound comes from anywhere forward of the beam of my steamer, I must at once get the way off my steamer" (so far the advice is sound), "that is to say, I should give the order to stop and reverse until my vessel has no longer way through the water." (This advice is unsound, as will presently appear. Recall, however, the author's statement that what he has written "is not a guide to seamanship," and reflect on what else such advice can possibly be.)

"I should *then* endeavour to localize the sound" (this is admirable), "and blowing my steam-whistle at constant intervals, should, *when the time comes to go ahead*, go dead slow, only just turning the engines over, and I should continue dead slow until I have felt my way past the danger."

If the words I have printed in italics were left out, this paragraph could hardly be improved in soundness, but the good has been marred, if not destroyed, by the context.

Moderate speed, and slackened speed, are properly prescribed in fog, (1) because a ship at slackened speed is more under command in virtue of the power held in reserve—especially in steamers. Generally speaking, ships can be stopped and turned in smaller spaces according as they have a reserve of power in hand; (2) the blow, if collision occurs, may be presumed to be less damaging.

But when a steam-ship with helm amidships stops and reverses, she nearly always escapes entirely from command. There is usually little guarantee which way her head will turn; it is nearly certain to turn one way or the other, and that may be the wrong way.* The dictum is as old as navigation itself that ships in company with others should not back sails except in the last extremity, and steam has strongly enforced the parallel order.

But our author misses the kernel of the question, which is this:—

The fog-signal of a ship under way, heard by a ship under way, necessarily proceeds from a ship which is doing or has done one of these several things—She has passed ahead; she has passed astern; she is about to pass ahead; she is about to pass astern; she is steering the same course, but parallel; she is steering an opposite course, but parallel; she is steering so as to arrive at some point which you are steering for also, and at which you will both arrive in nearly the same time. Evidently the latter must be the exceptional case, and yet it is the only one which necessitates any action on the part of the ship hearing the fog-signal.

If the sounder of the fog-signal is going to pass ahead in safety, say from starboard to port, the only things which can imperil that safety on the part of the hearing ship are *increased speed and starboard helm.* These are both movements tending to prevent the safe passage of the sounding ship. If, however, the ship sounding on the starboard side of the keel-line is not making to cross the bow at all, no alteration of the helm or speed is called for. Starboard helm to a fog-signal, heard to starboard, is therefore either dangerous or unnecessary. In like manner port helm to a fog-signal heard to port, is also dangerous or unnecessary. Increased speed is in both cases either dangerous or unnecessary.

The true teaching on hearing a fog-signal forward—both ships being under way—is therefore:—

(1) Slacken speed.

(2) Do not turn away from the sound.

These things are both legal and safe. The most dangerous thing which can be done is also, according to the records, the commonest. It is to combine a slackened speed with a turning

* On the other hand, she will obey her helm as with head way if it is put over before the engines are reversed.

away from the sound. The turning away is, in 99 cases out of 100, an effort to cross the bows of the other ship; the slackened speed frustrates that effort.*

What more should be done beyond the above preliminary steps will depend on whether the two ships are under the law, or under Article 23, where law by reason of the 'immediate danger' is abrogated. But this choice will only affect the ship which ought to 'keep her course' under the law. The other is already free in every way. Her acts ought to be the same in character whether the sound heard be near or far. The single advantage—if it is one—which the sound has over the light, is that it discloses generally its proximity or distance.

On such grounds we might advise the *steamer*, when there is any wind, hearing a *sailing vessel's* fog-horn forward—far or near—to slacken speed and turn to, but not beyond, the direction in which she first heard the sound. If the sailing ship is crossing her bows, the steamer by this movement helps her, and perhaps avoids a collision otherwise certain. If the sailing vessel is *not*

* I think that every case of collision in fog I have ever examined had a turning away from the sound in it on the part of one or both ships, and usually a slackened speed combined with it. It is so natural to turn away from a supposed danger, that in absence of sounder teaching this is not to be wondered at.

Thus the *Edith* hears a fog-signal on her port bow; ports, and slows her engines, and is run into on the port side and sank by the *Dordogne.*

The *Catherine Apcar* hears a steam-whistle on the port bow, ports, stops, and reverses, and is run into on the port side by the *Despatch.*

The *Kestrel* hears a steam-whistle on the port bow, ports, stops, and reverses, and is run into on her port side by the *Frankland.*

The *Vigilant* hears a steam-whistle on her port bow, ports, and stops her engines, and is run into on her port side by the *Hamburg.*

The *James Mason* hears a steam-whistle on her starboard bow, starboards, stops, and reverses, and runs into the port side of the *Llanelly*, &c., &c.

In a list of 29 consecutive fog cases tried in the Admiralty Court, 35 ships depose to turning away from the sound of a fog-signal, and only 10 depose to turning towards it. In only 2 cases did each ship depose to turning towards the other. In one of these, it is not possible that any such movements could have taken place at first, as may be understood on reference to Fig. 4. X deposes to seeing Y come out of the fog on her starboard bow, and to port helm thereupon. Y deposes to seeing X come out of the fog on her port bow, and to starboard helm thereupon. Yet both depose that the stem of Y struck the *starboard* bow of X, which could only happen if little or no helm movement had taken place. In the other case X deposes to keeping her helm hard a-port after seeing red change to green on her port bow, and to running into the starboard side of Y as a consequence.

crossing her bows, she will have moved away from the point to which the steamer is now steering.

The sailing vessel's duties towards the sailing vessel's fog-signal; and the steamer's duties towards the steamer's fog-signal, are not quite so clear. But I believe it would be legal, and it certainly would be as safe as any other course, for the ship which believes herself to be the 'giving way' ship, to give way by turning to, but not beyond, the point where the sound first proceeded from. The reasons for this course are the same as those just given, and the only special danger likely to arise, would be a mutual turning towards one another by the two ships, owing to apprehension of 'immediate danger,' or want of agreement as to which ship ought to keep her course. Everything, I know, tends to minimise the danger arising from this mutual, but limited, turn towards each other, and it certainly requires a number of concurrent circumstances, not likely to be found present, to make it an especial danger. It is certain that these movements seldom precede collisions in fog, while the contrary almost always do.

Our author goes on with a very good piece of advice:—"It is preferable that I should not alter my helm until I am fairly certain of the position of the other vessel," and then he immediately spoils it by adding:—"And, above all things, I must not act on the supposition that I am required by law to port my helm. I am certainly not required by law to port my helm, simply because I hear a whistle forward of my beam." This is exceedingly unsound doctrine, proceeding from want of comprehension of what the dangers of the port helm rule really were. The caution against port helm should only be given to the holding-on ship in the face of immediate danger. The fact is—and before the days of universal port helm it was usually taught—that port helm is the safe helm for the giving way ship in the large majority of cases. It is the proper helm for steamers giving way to steamers; it is the proper helm for sailing ships close hauled on the port tack giving way to sailing vessels on the starboard tack; it is generally the proper helm for the ship free on the starboard tack giving way to the ship close hauled on the port tack; and it is, in half the number of cases, the proper helm for the steamer giving way to the sailing vessel. The dictum in 1852 was not well put, and taken apart from the context, was erroneously read. It ran—"This doctrine is in harmony with the belief among seamen, that in all cases of doubt, the helm is to be ported."* It was not intended to say that port helm was a sort of trump card to be played in ignorance or despair; the context shows that owing to the incidence of the 'Rule of the Road,' port helm was generally right for the giving way ship, and it remains so, as we have seen. The danger of port helm was when it tended to take you across the bows of the other ship; and when it was universal, it usually did this for one of the two ships (see Fig. 4). There is no special vice in port helm any more than in starboard, and it is going beyond the requirements of the case, to say the least of it, to write as if there were. Probably the caution, if it is now required, ought not to extend further than to say that Article 15 does not apply when ships cannot see one another, as there is no means of knowing whether each is 'end on, or nearly end on' to the other.

Immediately after this, we light upon these words :—

"In the case of hearing a fog-horn, when I am in charge of a steamer in thick weather, I should stop, but should *not* reverse, until, in the words of the rules, I am satisfied that it is 'necessary,' as *if I reverse, control of the ship and helm would be lost. . . .*" It is terribly hard to know where we are with all this, and the ten thousand contradictory directions printed on opposite pages, and circulating through our mercantile marine.

A steam-whistle, we have been told, is a signal to reverse the engines, but a fog-horn is a signal *not* to reverse them, because then the control of the ship and helm would be lost. What is the meaning of it all? Is it a mere slip? But how is it possible to make such a slip on opposite pages? It is impossible to decide, and it is but a fresh instance of the oddity of the whole thing. But we cannot laugh at it only, seeing that the author has been a prominent member of all the recent Committees on the 'Rule of the Road'; that he is the head of the Marine Department of the Board of Trade; and that his views have been accepted by the

* 'The Rules of the Road, or Laws of Passing Vessels,' 1852, p. 17.

mercantile marine to the extent of ten thousand copies of his book, and two hundred and five thousand copies of his verses.

We must pass on now to some of the fundamental parts of the 'Rule of the Road,' and examine the teaching thereon which our author has so widely spread abroad. This brings us to section 10, "The holding-on ship," and the first question put under the section is, "When one of two ships is to keep out of the way, what is the other to do?" The first part of the answer given, is, "The other is *peremptorily* required to keep her course." Presently we are told, "I am *absolutely* required by law to keep my course, and I should therefore never alter it." Then a little lower down we have a weakened dictum:—

"I, being on board the 'holding-on' steam-ship, must only see that the other steamer does keep clear, but, *as a rule*, do nothing myself, except slow, stop, and reverse, if necessary, but only if necessary, . . . and although (under Article 18) I am to slow, stop, and reverse, if necessary, I am still to keep my course."

Such is the advice at the outset, and we are allowed our choice as to whether the law orders the 'holding-on ship' 'peremptorily,' 'absolutely,' or only 'as a rule' to keep her course. We may turn for enlightenment, if we feel at all troubled which gloss to choose, to the teaching current in 1852, taken from the same little manual already quoted. This is what is there laid down:—

"The Admiralty Judge has repeatedly declared it to be not merely the right, but also, in a certain sense, the duty of a vessel close-hauled meeting another free, or of a vessel close-hauled on the 'starboard tack' meeting another on a wind also, "to hold her course without deviation;" *but the privilege is not to be insisted upon when the existence of the right to use it admits of the slightest doubt.* It was decided . . . that as at night a vessel close-hauled on the port tack can never be quite sure whether a sail seen approaching her lee bow is close up to the wind, or a little from it, *it is the duty of the former to port her helm and bear away, even though the other may have the wind quite free.*"

The House of Lords, in the case of the *Europa* (steamer) and *Charles Bartlett* (sailing vessel) said:—

"The *Charles Bartlett*, it is to be observed, was under circumstances in which, according to the laws of navigation, she was entitled to keep her course. Of course it will not be understood that their lordships mean to lay down any rule, varying as it would from rules laid down before, and which are analogous to rules about keeping the road, such as are frequent at common law. Their lordships do not mean to lay down the rule that a ship, though entitled to keep her course, is to do so when under special circumstances it is obvious it will lead to, instead of avoiding, accident. All these general rules must be held to be rules bending to circumstances, but, *primâ facie*, a party entitled to keep his course has nothing else to do than to keep his course."

If we take these decisions, and compare them with the diagram in Fig. 4, we shall hardly fail to observe that the words of our author, 'peremptorily' and 'absolutely,' are false glosses, and highly dangerous. The other gloss, 'as a rule' is much nearer true teaching. Where the false teaching leads to, our author shows us lower down the page:—

"If I am sure that the other ship, which is required by law to keep out of my way, does not see me, or does not take steps to keep out of my way *until it appears to me to be too late,* then I must act."

Let those who follow me so far just think for a moment of ten thousand officers in charge of ships with this in their heads!

Of course, exactly opposite advice—that which has just been quoted—must be given if collision is to be avoided. The keeping of your course is only, 'in a certain sense,' a duty, and must not be persisted in if there is the slightest doubt as to its danger. We may be pretty sure that the House of Lords will not reverse its ruling in a matter of this kind.

No doubt the responsibility which the holding-on ship takes upon herself in choosing some action other than keeping her course, may be considerable; and one would suppose that a teacher believing the ship to be 'peremptorily' and 'absolutely' ordered to keep her course, and yet admitting a time when the order must be disobeyed, would be exceedingly careful to distinguish wrong acts from right acts in such a contingency. The question put:— "If I think the 'giving way' ship does not see me, what should I do, and why ?" would seem to lead directly to important and useful answers. But this is what we get :—

"Then I must act, and do what is necessary by slowing, stopping, going astern, or going ahead; throwing my ship in the wind, or putting the helm hard up, as may be necessary. . . . If I am in a sailing ship on a wind, and my ship is the holding-on ship, it will hardly ever be right for me to put my helm up; in the great majority of cases, if I am compelled to do anything, it will be better to put it down.

"If I am in a steam-ship, I can convey to the other ship by means of whistle-signals (that is, always bearing in mind that I can see her, or her lights), the fact that I intend to port or 'starboard' my helm, or go astern." *

So far as can be seen, there is no answer here to the question, "What should I do?" and certainly none to the further question, "Why should I do it?" There may be an exception in the case of the close-hauled ship, but why putting the helm down is safer for the holding-on ship than putting it up, we are not told.

Is it true of the modern rule of the road at sea, that when the holding-on ship determines to act in not keeping her course, &c., you can only say she should "do what is necessary?" Will she be better able to do what is necessary on the spur of the moment, and without any settlement beforehand what class of movements are generally safe, and what class are generally dangerous? The author seems to think so, but I doubt if the courts agree with him.

We have just had the very different and less modern teaching put before us. We were told in 1852 that when the ship close-hauled on the port tack being possibly the 'holding-on' ship to a possibly free ship approaching on her lee bow, "she was, when in doubt, to put her helm up and bear away, even though the other might have the wind quite free."

The principle involved here is clear enough. It was the duty of the free ship on the starboard tack to 'give way' to, that is, to make for a point astern of, the ship close-hauled on the port tack.

* As, however, by Art. 19, a steam-ship can only signal such movements as are "authorised or required by these regulations," the use here proposed is probably illegal.

If the ship on the port tack had any doubt as to her fulfilling that duty, then she herself was to make for passing astern of the ship free on the starboard tack.

In general terms, there must not be a struggle for precedence, but there may be a struggle to surrender a right.

The soundness of this teaching is confirmed by the fact that collisions are very commonly preceded by a struggle for precedence, and very rarely by a struggle to surrender the right of way. The reason of this is very fairly disclosed in Fig. 4.

In still plainer terms, the seaman may be told that if the giving-way ship is trying to cross his bows, he may try to pass under her stern, but he must not try, by any alteration of course, to force himself across her bows.

What plain common sense this is, and what a satisfactory answer to our author's question!. .Why could he not give it himself?

But we may look at the matter a little more closely in order to see how, if the seamen of a past age were right in their principles, how very right those principles are now.

Suppose, in the case just quoted, that the ships had coloured lights, and it was night. The ship on the port tack would see the *red* light of the approaching starboard-tacked ship, and the latter would see the *green* light of the port-tacked ship. By the hypothesis, the starboard-tacked ship is either not going to put her helm up at all, or she is delaying, and the danger is growing. Supposing the port-tacked ship—believing himself to be the holding-on ship, which is also the hypothesis—has in his mind our author's teaching, "that it will hardly ever be right for him to put his helm up," will he not certainly keep a close luff as a preliminary?

Examine Fig. 3, and see whether the danger will not grow steadily? What is the result as regards the ship on the starboard tack? She had a *green* light in view to begin with, and she has seen no change in it, no more warning after the close luff than before the close luff. But if there was a doubt about crossing the port-tacked ship's bows before the close luff, there may be more doubt after it; though that is not made known to the starboard-tacked ship. Presently the danger has become imminent, and the port-tacked ship, still full of our author's dictum, puts his helm down, and throws himself into collision across the bows of the starboard-tacked ship. Remark here, that this is the usual type of sailing ship collisions, either on the part of one ship, or of the other.

Now take the old seamanship of the case. The port-tacked ship would have had just the opposite dictum in his mind. The Trinity Masters had told him that 'he must *never* put his helm a-lee'—he must *never* do what our author says he should do in the 'majority of cases.'

Thinking that the *red* light is carried by a free ship, and that he is 'to keep his course'—but 'not to insist' on his right of way, and yet observing a growing danger, he puts his helm up to the 'quite free' starboard-tacked ship. His action is clearly signalled to the starboard-tacked ship by the change of his lights as shown, from *green* to *green* and *red*, and then to *red* only—the safety signal.

Hence we can safely and distinctly answer our author's question in terms of the lights, by saying that at night, "If I, being in the holding-on ship, think that the 'giving way' ship does not see me, and that there will be danger in persisting in my right to keep my course, I should obey the signal made by his lights. That is to say, I should port to a *red* light, or starboard to a *green* light."

Note here, that this is a case governed by Article 23, the 'immediate danger' clause, and that therefore there is no 'law' to govern it. It becomes a question of pure seamanship. There are cases of very close proximity, where in certain particular positions, porting to a *red* light, or starboarding to a *green* light, could not be distinctly recommended. Such cases are in so small a minority that they may be neglected; and, moreover, when they arise, there are almost certainly other clear indications beside the mere appearance, direction, and change of direction of the coloured light. They are all cases of converging courses, say one ship steering N., and another to starboard steering N.W., &c. The proximity must be very close before danger can arise from obeying the light-signals.

Note again, that stopping and reversing engines, or backing sails, will always be right when porting to a *red* light, or starboarding to a *green* one, and always wrong when using the opposite movements.

Section 11 of our author's book deals with the proposition, "One ship is to keep out of the way," and the questions on it are various. "When do I port at once? In what cases do I first wait a sufficient time before doing anything? Why should I then make up my mind, and act on it soon? What will be the consequence of unnecessary delay on my part? If two steamers are crossing at this angle , how can the position be most readily converted into one of safety, and by which ship? What must a giving way steamer never neglect?"

Here are a goodly array of questions to which plain answers might reasonably be expected. Let us turn to the section for them. As to the first question of the series, we are told:—"I must port at once if I see both side-lights ahead, or nearly ahead; but if I see only one side-light anywhere, I must not port or starboard at once, unless the vessels are very close, which may happen in thick weather?"

On this advice we have to ask, why has the author brought the port helm rule into the discussion of the case where '*one*' ship only is to act? He has already told us, in a former section, that it had nothing to do with such a case; and it is of course foreign matter. But passing this by, where do we get the law or the seamanship which tells us that we must port 'at once' to both coloured lights, but 'not at once' to a single light, though it may be proper to do it after a pause? There is no such distinction anywhere in the rules. A *red* or a *green* light alone is more or less of a permanent signal, not likely to change, and generally conveying the same order to you—if it conveys any order to you—the moment you see it clearly, as it does after a pause. Both coloured lights form a very temporary signal, possibly conveying to you the exact opposite of what it appears on a momentary glance to convey. It would appear that the caution ought to be the other way, and that it is more important to pause before porting to both coloured lights ahead, than to pause before porting to (say) a *red* light a little on the starboard bow.

Perhaps the answer to the second question is more correctly given, if the law of port helm had not been imported into it:

"I must generally watch the light a bit, and then act in good time. I must not leave the other ship in doubt, or she will think I do not see her, and then her master may do something wrong."

The partial failure of such advice has been already adverted to at p. 12b. That is to say, it might lead a student to think that he ought to make some pause after he has ascertained all three possible conditions of the case :—(1) the colour of the light; (2) its direction; (3) whether it is altering its direction. Whereas not a moment's pause should be made after these things are known. The only object—as before explained—of waiting after the colour of the light has been determined, and danger more or less remote indicated thereby, is to note the amount of change of bearing, and thus to avoid an unnecessary movement. But little harm can come of the giving way ship instantly porting to a *red* light, or instantly starboarding to a *green*, provided it is certain that the colours are really *red*, or really *green*.

Following this advice, which can be thus only partially approved, we come on advice almost altogether to be commended :—

"If two sailing ships are crossing with the wind on different sides, and it is necessary for the one of them that is to keep out of the way to alter her course to avoid collision, it will, as a rule, be proper for her to pass astern of the other; at all events, she should never attempt to cross ahead of the track of the ship that is required by law to keep her course." It is evident that if she should "never attempt to cross ahead," she must always attempt to pass astern, and the term just used, 'as a rule,' has no fit place in the paragraph. Thus our author finds himself merely repeating what the courts laid down in years gone by, and which has only been weakened by more recent decisions on an altered phrase of law. If only he could have seen that this is a truth, not only for two sailing ships with the wind on different sides, but for all ships in all conditions under the law! And if ten thousand copies of this undiluted truth had been spread abroad instead of the curious mixture of opposites contained in this book—well! a good many ships would be at the surface now instead of at the bottom of the sea!

The answer to the question about steamers is :—

"If two steamers are crossing at an oblique angle, and I am on board the steamer that is to keep out of the way, I can generally convert that position of danger into one of safety by showing my own *red* light to my opponent's *red* light; but in most other cases, it is safe to shape my course to pass astern."

Here again the advice is quite sound, but odd. He has really said, "A steamer should always port to a steamer's red light to starboard." But he does not appear to think he has said so. Indeed if we turn to p. 43, and read :—

> "If to my starboard *red* appear,
> It is my duty to keep clear;
> To act as judgment says is proper,
> To port, *or starboard*, back or stop her,"

we see it is almost certain that he cannot think he has contradicted his prose by his rhyme. To reconcile them, he should have written :—

> "To act as judgment says is proper,
> To port the helm, and back, or stop her."

But in the irreconcileable difference between the prose advice and the rhyming advice, we are left to decide which is right. Porting to a red light to starboard is always "shaping my course to pass astern," and nothing else; while starboarding to the same light is always "shaping my course to pass ahead." The author has printed ten thousand copies of his prose advice that it is safe for me to "shape my course to pass astern," but he has printed two hundred and five thousand copies of his rhyming advice that the matter is one of indifference—"You are to shape your course to pass astern, *or ahead,* whichever you choose."

After what has gone before it is needless to repeat. But we may conclude this part of the subject by the soundest advice in the book, given at p. 41.

"Never forget, that if you port to a *green* light ahead or on your port bow, or starboard to a *red* light ahead or on your starboard bow, YOU ARE DOING YOUR BEST TO GET INTO COLLISION."

I have only been able to get one explanation for these distinctly contradictory utterances on the fundamental principle of all rules of the road by our author. I imagine he may think—(1) that unless the *green* or the *red* light is seen very far forward indeed, it may be right to use the helm opposite to that which he recommends in his prose ; and (2) he may think that lights of ships under way, as seen from a steamer under way, are equally distributed all round the horizon. That therefore it is a pretty even chance whether it is right for the giving way ship to port or starboard to a *red* light.' The transparent plates accompanying this little book, and which give the manœuvring powers of the best and worst manœuvring ships, doing what they are capable of in the way of manœuvring, will, if superposed on one another clearly show where the truth lies in the one assumption ; while the ascertained fact that in collision cases at night, in 93 out of every 100, the lights are first seen less than 4 points from the line of keel, on either bow, ought to settle matters with the other.

Section 14 deals with Article 20 of the "Regulations for preventing collisions at sea," which is in the following terms: "Notwithstanding anything contained in any preceding article every ship, whether a sailing-ship or a steam-ship overtaking any other, shall keep out of the way of the overtaken ship."

Our author's first question is, "What does Dr. Johnson define overtaking to be." But we might justly doubt whether any general definition by Dr. Johnson would help us much with technical 'overtaking' as defined in sea law. And in fact, we do not seem to advance much by learning that, "to overtake is to catch anything by pursuit ; to come up with something going before." The real difficulty is to define what is 'overtaking' as used in this article in the eye of the law, and it must then be remembered that the two highest maritime courts differed (in the case of the *Franconia*) as to what was 'overtaking.' The difficulty is that 'overtaking' (Article 20) merges into 'approaching' (Article 14) ; into 'crossing' (Article 16) ; and "proceeding in such directions as to involve risk of collision" (Article 17) ; and that the order for 'overtaking' may be directly contrary to the order for the other cases. The further difficulty is that at night one ship has the power under this article of commanding the other ship, though the other ship has no order to obey such command. Any ship at night may announce, by showing a white light astern, that she claims the right of way, but the ship seeing the light is nowhere ordered to obey it, and may, in spite of it, claim to have *her* right of way—which is the kind of silent dispute which generally ends in collision. The showing of a stern light was long suggested as proper before it was legalized. But it does not appear that those who suggested it meant that it should assert any special right which might be disputed by an approaching ship.

The difficulty immediately developed itself by converting the word 'overtaking' into 'faster,' and the word 'overtaken' into 'slower.' And the committee of 1877 thought that there was 'every reason' why the faster ship should be compelled to yield to the slower ship, while the slower ship kept her course. But 'faster' and 'slower' do not seem to be properly convertible terms with 'overtaking' and 'overtaken.' Possibly the committee had in their minds a proposition such as:—"There is every reason why a ship astern of, or on either quarter of another ship, and coming up with her, should, if necessary, alter course so as not to run the first ship down." Our author expresses very nearly this view, and perhaps, if it stood alone, we might accept it. But the whole difficulty is that it does not stand alone. For instance, a faster steamer coming up 'abaft the starboard beam' of another steamer, which therefore bears upon her port bow, is, under Mr. Gray's interpretation of Article 22, 'peremptorily' ordered to keep her course. But the other steamer observing the first steamer approaching on her starboard beam, is, according to the same interpretation of the same article, 'peremptorily' ordered to keep her course. There is no possible way of deciding between these two ships, and the regulations so far fail to get the mutual understanding between them which they have been established to secure. So, as before said, we not only have ships disputing over the point in the absence of full information, but the two highest courts dispute over the same point.

Our author does not touch on this, the only point which appears to require touching on, but assumes a distinction between 'crossing' and 'overtaking' which is at best very difficult indeed to arrive at. It is the more remarkable that he should neglect it, as it is only under teaching such as he supplies that the danger is great. This can arise only from an idea of the 'peremptoriness' or 'absoluteness' of the order to 'keep your course.' If the old teaching be in vogue, there will be more tendency to yield than to persevere, and less danger as a consequence.

It is, however, not unlikely—indeed there is much reason to believe—that the stern light is even now becoming permanent. It is much easier to keep it always displayed, and be safe, than to keep it, as our author says, 'in a bucket, or quite handy,' and to have some one stationed to show it as long as lights are seen astern. In this case the stern light may be generally accepted as a sort of 'not under command' signal, making all who see it feel the onus of avoiding it, without any distinct reference to the 'overtaking' clause.

Speaking of the case as regards the overtaking clause at night, our author practically follows the ruling of the Judicial Committee of the Privy Council in the case of the *Franconia*, which was given before the establishment of the stern light, and might possibly be altered by that fact, he says:—

"What I understand is, that if two ships are approaching each other, and the side-light of one is opposed to the side-light of the other, the two ships are crossing ships, and the crossing rules apply."

"But when I am coming up with a ship going before, and we are in such relative positions that I should, at night, be abaft the range (the arc) of her side-lights, I am to regard myself, with certainty, as an overtaking ship, and I am to keep out of the way of the one going before."

I am not sure that the Privy Council decision pressed the case so far as this; and, as before stated, the establishment of the stern light may alter their decision in future cases. But if this is right law and teaching, seamen certainly want a good many cautions about it. In brief it comes to this, that if you are approaching another ship in a direction $1\frac{1}{2}$ points abaft her beam, you are a 'crossing ship,' but if you are approaching $2\frac{1}{2}$ points abaft her beam, you are an 'overtaking ship.' And if you are in a steamer approaching a steamer on her starboard side, you are to do exactly the opposite in the one case to what you are to do in the other.

A good deal of caution is certainly necessary. The seaman

approaching abaft the beam of the other ship should certainly be warned that with so indefinite a boundary between opposing laws, differences of opinion are certain. It does not follow that because I, in a steamer, see on my port bow the stern light and the green light of another steamer which I am approaching, that therefore the other steamer will admit me to be a 'crossing ship,' and give me the right of way. Nay, if his stern light is not permanent, I have got a signal that he does not admit, and will not give me my right of way. Again, if I only see his stern light, it does not follow that he will consider me an 'overtaking' ship, unless I am certain that the stern light has been specially shown for me. I may be within the arc, but beyond the range, of his coloured side-light.

Again, the seaman requires to be warned about this very doubtful and difficult position. "Having considered yourself an overtaking ship in the absence of sight of a coloured side-light, are you still such when the coloured light comes into view?"

Looking to the probability of the white stern light becoming permanent—merely to save time and trouble—it will be better for fast ships seeing the white light to proceed with caution (remembering the four or five other things represented by white light), and then to determine by its motion to right or left, whether to starboard or port, or if a side-light comes into view, to obey the signal made by it. But of all things, to recollect that in no case is there a 'peremptory' order to 'keep your course.'

Section 15 in our author's book is "An introductory statement to the next section," which goes into cases and particulars under the sailing 'Rules of the Road' (Article 14). He here lays it down that the principle that the ship most qualified keep out of the way, should keep out of the way of the other, "forms the foundation of the rules." The statement is the more remarkable as appearing at p. 48 of the ed. of 1878, after the following, at p. 23:—

"This creature" (an absurd little sketch of a steam-launch),—"which I may explain is a steam 'ship'—is required to keep out of the way of all sailing ships, large as well as small; but if she has the *Great Eastern* on her own port-side, and is a crossing ship, then, if you please, the *Great Eastern* is to get out of her way. This ship" (an absurd little lugger)—"which I may mention is a sea-going 'ship,' that is to say, a lugger not propelled by oars—holds her way against all steamers, large and small, and against all other sailing ships, where under the rules she is the holding-on ship . . . ."

The first statement may approach the truth in a majority of cases in ships otherwise equal, but the ridicule the author throws on his own statement carries away probably the larger share of the truth. We have seen (p. 28) how in equal steamers the relative nearness to the collision point makes all the difference in the power of getting out of the way; and our author shows us how mere difference in size may utterly swallow up all other differences in relative powers of manœuvring. There is clearly more behind this question than need be entered on here, and we may pass on to a few brief remarks on his mode of treating sailing ship rules amongst themselves.

He gives us a list in which each sailing ship gives way to all below in the list, and keeps her course to all ships above her in the list. Thus :—

(*a*) Wind aft.
(*b*) Free port side.
(*c*) Free starboard side.
(*p*) Close-hauled port tack.
(*s*) Close-hauled starboard tack.

Which is no doubt correct if it be remembered that all is reversed where the holding-on ship is 'overtaking.'

But then our author says nothing about the real difficulties, namely, as to the limits between 'close-hauled' and 'free'; 'free' and 'wind aft.' These are the points on which disputes arise, and where the student might reasonably wish for simpler and plainer law without niceties, the attempt to balance which has led to collision.

Where is the distinction between 'wind aft' and 'free' in view of keeping your course, or altering it? Does 'aft' mean exactly right aft?—or does it mean yards square? Is wind 3 points on the quarter 'free' or 'aft'? Where is the limit? Is steering a course 'clean full' and yards sharp, 'close-hauled' or 'free'? If the ship is steering 'full and bye,' no doubt she is close-hauled, even though strong wind and reduced sail prevent her from lying nearer than 8 points of the wind. But I suppose disputes have arisen even over that point.

A main difficulty was touched upon but not pursued by Dr. Lushington, when, in 1859, the proposal that sailing ships should carry coloured lights as at present was under debate. It is that at night the coloured light is a clearer signal than the direction of the wind, as to how a sailing ship seen is steering. And though our author speaks as if there were only one case where this conflict of signals occurs at night, there are in fact plenty of cases. Whether to obey the more certain signal of the light seen, or the less certain signal of the wind's direction, is a nightly question in thousands of ships. Our author gives his doubtful case, and says there is "no system by which the difficulty can be done away with," not perceiving that the difficulty only arises because the law may say one thing when the light says another, and that if law said what light said, there would be an end of it.

But while light and law do not always say the same things, it becomes a necessity to tell the seaman what is best under the circumstances; and what we ought to say seems to be this, which is applicable to all cases under all the rules.

"Endeavour by every means in your power to make certain of your position; but if a doubt remains—give way. Port your helm and stop your way to a *red* light. Starboard your helm and stop your way to a *green* light, whenever such lights point at danger."

We have now finished with our author, whose work must be seriously taken on account of its very wide circulation. That which is sound in it I have commended. That which is demonstrably wrong I have condemned, because apart from such condemnation, it is calculated to breed disaster.

CHAPTER III.

THE MANŒUVRING POWERS OF SHIPS AS RELATING TO COLLISION AT SEA.

NOT only as the proper foundation of all rules of the road at sea, but quite apart from law, and merely as the seamanship concerned in avoiding collision, I have shown in the preceding chapters, how important a knowledge of the manœuvring powers of ships is. The transparent diagrams in the cover of this book, give a general idea of the manœuvring powers of steam-ships more complete than has yet been published, and may be relied on to express the general powers possessed by ships of all classes.

The ship T has powers probably far above the average; the ship E powers probably rather below the average; and the ship F has powers certainly below the average—for men-of-war. It may be assumed that the average for men-of-war is higher than that for the mercantile marine, and that therefore the ships of that service cannot be credited with greater powers than those shown in the transparent diagrams.

Manœuvring powers consist in powers of turning, and losing and gathering way. Generally, seamen must be credited with a belief that these powers are greater than they are really found to be when tested by actual trial. In turning, for instance, with especial reference to avoiding collision, it seems to be very generally supposed that a ship, on putting her helm over, begins immediately to pass away to the right or left of the course she would have pursued had her helm not been touched. The diagrams show that this is so far from being the case, that even with the handiest ship, ship T, she must turn some three points of the compass before her stern will clear the original path she was pursuing. This point at which the original path begins to be cleared is nearly two lengths ahead of the ship T, and in worse manœuvrers, ships E and F, it is still further off. Nor even with the twin-screw T developing turning power to an extent not probably exceeded in any sea-going ship, is this power of clearing the original path greatly enhanced.

Altering course, the diagrams show us, is not—so far as manœuvring to avoid collision goes—the same thing as altering the direction of the ship's head. Looking at No. 1, ship E, we can see that, supposing she were steering North, and her helm is put hard over till she is apparently steering N.E. by E. ½ E., she has really steered somewhere about N. by E. only, since she started; and it has taken her a distance of more than 4 times her length to do it in; or, in a ship 300 feet long, no less than 400 yards. In the ship F, which is a worse manœuvrer, it takes six points of alteration in direction of ship's head, to make one and a half points real alteration of course; and it takes her a distance of nearly seven times her length to do it in. If she were 300 feet long, and saw a fixed object, such as a ship at anchor, 600 yards off, and a point and a half on her bow, she would run into it in her attempt to clear it with 32° of helm. The ship T is one of the handiest ships that have yet been found, yet she must alter the direction of her head some five and a half points, to effect a real alteration of course of about a point; and it takes her nearly four times her length to do it in. If she employs her twin-screws in their utmost development of her manœuvring power, she hardly really alters course at all when changing the direction of her head as much as eight points.

These are all space measurements. The results of the time measurements are quite as striking. It has taken the ship E 85 seconds to go as far in a N. by E. direction as it would have taken her only 65 seconds to go steering North. If she wanted to cross a line 400 yards in front of her, it would take her 25 per cent. longer to do it with her helm over to 30° than with it amidships. The ship T would lose 14 per cent. in time of crossing a line 300 yards ahead of her if she put her helm over. The ship F would lose less in turning, but this is simply because she would effect no real alteration of her course by putting her helm over to cross a line three lengths in front of her.

In all ships tried, it has been found that the speed begins to fall very soon after the helm is put over. In turning through the first 4 points, the mean speed is not so much affected as it is during the second 4 points of the turn; and then the mean speed over the third and fourth 'octants,' as we now call them, does not greatly differ, though it is somewhat lower than the mean speed over the second octant. The great change in fact takes place during the turn of 8 points, after which there is not much change of any kind either in speed, or in the rate at which the ship's head alters its direction. It invariably takes longer to turn through the first octant than through the second; and usually a ship turns more quickly through the second octant than through any other. So far as the avoidance of collision goes, the transparent diagrams show that what happens after the ship has turned 5 or 6 points is not of importance.

The powers a ship has of checking or increasing her way through the water are more open to variation than her powers of turning. The full helm angle is a fixed amount, and putting the helm over to any given angle has practically in sea-going ships precisely the same effect whether the speed is great or small. Even if the engines are stopped when the helm is put over in a steam-ship, the effect is nil except on the speed.

Reversing the engines in a single screw ship, or both engines in a twin-screw ship, has practically little effect if the helm is first put over, no matter at what point of the turn it is done. A slight effect on decreasing the radius of the arc over which the ship turns is the only change to be expected beside the reduction of speed, until the ship has nearly lost head-way. But few ships will turn more than 4 points if the order to put the helm over, and to reverse the engines, be given simultaneously. But the ship will *invariably* in such cases obey the helm as with head-way for some time. No greater results in checking way in a single-screw ship can be got than by the simultaneous use of helm and reversed engines. The transparent diagram No. 4 is a good example of the best that can be done in a ship going 12 knots with a good head of steam, but not a reserve of steam, by putting the helm over and reversing the engines. If this diagram is laid over No. 1 so that the ships coincide, some idea will be given of the comparatively limited powers of checking way possessed by a steam-ship at speed.

It comes practically to this, that if we suppose a line drawn at right angles across the path of E, 275 yards from her bow, at a time when E is going 12 knots, she may, by putting her helm over and reversing her engines full speed, extend the time in which she would otherwise have reached it by about 75 per cent. If the ship going on would have reached the line in 40 seconds she may be delayed for 30 seconds more by putting the helm hard over and reversing. But she still has some way left, and will cross the line a little later. A handier ship, like T, using her twin screws as in No. 5, could altogether stop short of the line which the other would pass, while neither ship without the assistance of the helm could do so much towards checking way.

It may be observed that it is highly probable that the movement of a sailing ship in wearing corresponds to that of a steam-ship with her helm over. While the action of a sailing ship in tacking must closely resemble T in diagram 5.

Time and space, it will be seen, enter into the measure of every sort of manœuvring power; and in all questions of avoiding collision, time is the question whenever there is a crossing of paths, either curved or straight. Space alone is concerned when either ship is able by any manœuvre, however prolonged in time, to avoid touching or crossing the path of the other ship. As in Fig. 4, for instance, time and space are both concerned if Y in the endeavour to avoid X, does not put her helm a-starboard. If neither ship does anything, it is a question of time alone whether X is able to pass ahead of Y, or Y is able to pass ahead of X in safety. If it takes Y nine of X's intervals of time to reach the crossing-point, X will be just able to pass in safety. But if X's intervals were 6 seconds, while Y's were 5 seconds, X would be run down. If X puts her helm a-starboard and Y keeps her course, it will still be a question of time only, whether collision will or will not be avoided. But the act of X in putting her helm a-starboard is such as to delay her progress across the path of Y. If she had let her helm alone, and the time intervals were equal for both ships, she would have been clear across the path of Y in 9 intervals; but if she had put her helm a-starboard, she would still be lying across the path of Y in 9 intervals, and Y would have run her down. If she had put her helm a-port, her stern would still be across the path of Y in 9 intervals, but then she would have gained a little time, inasmuch as the bow of Y would not reach the new crossing-point until about half an interval later. So also will it be a question of time if Y ports and X does either of the three things open to her. If the speeds are equal or nearly so, X may just escape if she keeps her course, but cannot escape for want of time if she puts her helm either way.

But if Y puts her helm a-starboard, the question of time does not arise at all. It does not in the least affect the chances of collision whether Y is going faster or slower than X.

If we take diagram No. 1, and suppose E steering West, and then take the other diagram No. 1, and place the 9th interval on the straight course of the latter, coincident with the 9th interval of the former, and suppose the upper E to be steering North; we see that it is not possible for the upper E to avoid a crossing of the lower E's original course. We also see that while the upper E's bow will be on the lower E's path in 9 intervals if she keeps her helm steady, her bow will not be up to it till after 11 intervals if she puts her helm either way.

Now if the intervals are equal for both ships—that is in this case, if they are at equal speeds—there must be collision at the crossing-point of the straight courses, in 9 intervals of time. Supposing the upper E to be anxious to do her best to avoid a collision, and that she knows that as there must be a crossing somewhere, the question is one of time only, what should she do?

There is the first choice. Shall she try to pass ahead of the lower E, or to let the lower E pass ahead of her? Let us say she chooses the former, and then follows an increase of speed as a measure certainly called for. What powers has she of doing this?

Her bow is about three lengths from the crossing-point, and she must be more than one length further advanced if she is to clear the crossing-point before the lower E reaches it. That is to say, she must increase her mean speed by more than one-third. Of course she cannot do this if she is anywhere near the full speed due to the boilers in use. If she is not near that full speed, then she must have a boiler power in reserve of more than one-third. But supposing she has this, which is exceedingly improbable, time is required for its development. She cannot spring instantly from 9 to 12 knots, nor from 12 to 16, nor even from 3 to 4 knots. An order must be given and obeyed; the immediate draft upon the steam by the opening of the throttle-valve must be met by opening draught-plates and firing up. After the full pressure of the steam has been brought to bear, the inertia of the ship has to be overcome and balanced—all of which takes further time. If these ships were going 12 knots, the time at disposal is 45 seconds only. If 6 knots, 90 seconds, and so on. It is abundantly clear that with ordinary ships there is not the slightest chance for the upper E to clear the path of the lower E by passing ahead of her on a straight course.

Let us suppose now, that abandoning the idea of doing anything with increase of speed in the time, the upper E puts her helm hard a-starboard. The result we see is, that after 11 intervals of time she has still failed even to reach the crossing-point. So far, the movement has had exactly the opposite effect to that intended, for the lower E's 11th interval of time is not coincident with, but a-head of, that of the upper E. If then there would have been a failure, by attempted increase of speed, to force the upper E across the bows of the lower E, it will only be still more marked if any attempt had been made to combine it with starboard helm.

Port helm for the upper E is clearly not a movement to pass ahead of, but is a movement to pass astern of, the lower E. Hence a combination of increased speed with port helm would be that of two opposites, and it follows that we have discussed everything which it is open to the upper E to do in her endeavour to pass ahead of the lower E, and we should gather that all such endeavours are futile.

Suppose that the upper E believing this, were to manœuvre to let the lower E pass ahead of her. Reduction of speed is here as plain a demand as increase was in the other case. The powers of reducing the way of a steam-ship through the water, though very limited, as we have seen, are yet *primâ facie* greater than the powers of increasing it. For first, while it is only the reserve power which can be employed to increase speed, it is the whole power plus any reserve there may be, which is available to reduce speed through the water. But in the case before us, the speed of the upper E must be reduced in the inverse proportion of 9 to nearly 13 if she keeps her course, in order to let the lower E pass ahead of her. And though it be admitted that the power of reducing speed be greater than the power of increasing it, it remains questionable whether it is great enough to effect the object in the time. At least it is worth while examining how far the helm may be made to assist.

Omitting reduced speed, then, let us note what helm alone can do in this case. We have seen that by putting the helm over either way, the crossing of the straight path of lower E is delayed; and as delay is just what is wanted, it would certainly be proper to put it over either way, and the only remaining question is, which way? What is wanted is to delay the arrival of the upper E, and, if it be possible, to hasten the arrival of the lower E, at the crossing-point. Starboard helm for the upper E certainly delays the arrival of the upper E, but it also delays the arrival of the lower E at the crossing-point, and so only reduces the chances of collision in a certain degree. Port helm, however, for the upper E has a different effect. In 11 intervals of time, if the upper E ports her helm even without any reduction of speed, the danger of collision is passed; as in 7 intervals of time the lower E has reached a point which the upper E cannot reach until more than 11 intervals have elapsed. Any reduction of speed which the upper E can effect in addition to that due to her helm, is only making assurance doubly sure, and increasing the least distance at which the ships can approach one another.

Now, in order to see that we are not misled by the fact that we are dealing with two equal ships at equal speeds, we can apply No. 2, the ship T, steering North, in the same way to the ship E, steering West.

The relative conditions, it may at once be seen, are just the same;

but the speed of T being so much less than that of E, she is correspondingly nearer to the crossing-point, and has correspondingly less power to avoid collision by any means whatever. Yet do her best chances lie in port helm and reduced speed. Like conditions again obtain if ship F is used in place of the upper ship E. Her manœuvring powers are worse, and therefore her chances of avoiding collision are diminished, but the relative value of the different manœuvres remains the same. No. 4 diagram shows what E can do in the way of reducing her speed. If the orders to put the helm over, and to reverse the engines, are given simultaneously, the ship will turn in the times and spaces given. That is to say, that this power of reversing gives to her a very considerable margin of safety if she uses port helm. If we use No. 5 in the same way, we see that if there are only 9 intervals of time for each ship's reaching the crossing-point—that is, if E's speed is 12 knots, and T's $6\frac{1}{2}$ knots, then it is not in the power of T to avoid a collision if E keeps her course and speed, notwithstanding the very superior manœuvring powers which the use of her twin screws give her. But still the relative advantages of the different manœuvres open to her, remain the same; if we put her 11 intervals off the crossing-point, she can easily avoid collision by port helm and reversed starboard screw. If she is a little further off still—say 13 intervals—there is no crossing at all if she reverses the inner screw and puts the helm over, as she has the power of turning either way, short of the path of E.

Thus, widely differing ships and conditions might be multiplied to any extent, but the same general principles would always obtain.

If we apply No. 1, ship E, to the other ship E, as at first, we shall see this: that collision may be avoided by mutual acts of the two ships. If both ships port their helms there will be just time enough for the lower E to pass ahead of the upper E. This will be the case also so long as the upper E reduces her speed, provided the lower E does not reduce hers still more. In the same way there will be no collision if both starboard. So also will there be no collision if the upper E starboards, and the lower E ports, no matter how they deal with their speed. But there will most probably be collision if the upper E ports and the lower E starboards; and it is a broad and loose conception of the danger of this latter pair of movements and the safety of the former pair, which leads seamen to such constant applications of wrong helm.

It is perfectly true that in this case it is much more dangerous for the two ships to turn *towards*, than to turn *from*, each other, but this follows only because the ships are in all respects equal. If we apply ship T as before, either with or without the reversal of her starboard screw, we see that if the ships turn tow ardone another it is almost impossible for them to come into collision. So with ship F. Even should she continue to keep her helm a-port, she will cross the bow of E clear of her. So will it be with the upper E if she reverses; and in short the only reason why the mutual turn towards each other is dangerous is because of a series of equalities almost impossible to arise between two ships at sea.

But one of the reasons which have assisted in producing this whole series of conclusions, is, that the courses of the ships cross at right angles, and consequently the shortest distance to the crossing is the course either ship is steering. Let us, therefore, vary the circumstances by supposing different courses, and let the lower ship E (No. 1) be steering West, and the upper E (No. 1) be steering North-East, the crossing-point being 9 intervals ahead of each ship as before.

The first thing we note is, that the ships are much further apart than they were before (between 600 and 700 yards), and therefore the possibilities of avoiding collision should be by so much greater. Yet collision will come about if either of five things are done: *i. e.* (1) if both ships keep their courses; (2) if upper E keeps her course, and lower E ports; (3) if lower E keeps her course, and upper E starboards; (4) if the ships turn away from each other; (5) if the ships turn towards each other. So far as helm is concerned, then, collision will only be avoided if one of the two ships keeps her course, and the other turns towards her. The circumstances in fact involve the general case, and show the wisdom of the old law. It would prescribe that one ship (say the lower E) should keep her course, and the other (say the upper E) should port her helm. She would be forbidden to starboard her helm, for the very plain reason, that, if she does, she will present her broadside as nearly as possible at right angles to receive the blow of the lower E's stem.

If we move upper E two intervals further off, and place her 11th interval over the 9th of the lower E, we shall assume a speed of 11 for upper E and 9 for lower E, and make no other change. Then we see that if lower E keeps her course, it is still fatal for upper E to starboard, but safe for her to port. It is, however, safe for upper E to starboard, *provided* lower E either ports or starboards. It looks at first just as dangerous as before for the ships to turn towards each other, but it is not so in reality, for in 4 intervals only of lower E's time, upper E will have made the safety signal to her, either by opening her masts in daylight, or showing her red light at night, so giving lower E ample time and space to right her helm.

Now, if we go on moving upper E round so that her course shall grow more and more nearly opposite to that of lower E, we shall see that the danger of starboard helm for upper E hardly grows less on the understanding that lower E will keep her course; while it continually grows greater on the understanding that lower E will port. Port helm, on the other hand, only grows more and more safe for upper E no matter what lower E does, for the latter gets the safety signal correspondingly earlier. And then, the same law—were it properly drawn—which gave lower E the right to continue her course across the bows of upper E, under the original conditions, would forbid her to continue starboard helm tending to take her across the bows of upper E under the changed conditions. These are points of seamanship and possible law, which are so little understood that I find it generally requires quite an effort to master them.

If we apply ship T with the 45° crossing angle to ship E and the 9th intervals coincident, the conditions are so far changed that we have another state such that if E does not turn towards T, collision is certain. But if we go on moving T back—supposing her speed to increase proportionately—we only develop the same conditions as we had before. And it is the same if we go on decreasing the crossing angle. The danger of starboard helm for T goes on increasing on the understanding that E keeps her course; while the safety of port helm for T goes on increasing on the understanding that E keeps her course or ports, and its danger goes on decreasing on the supposition that E starboards, because of the earlier notice she gets by the safety signal.

The same general results follow the application of F to E, except that being a ship so much smaller, she is able to get herself across the course of the other in a shorter time, and might escape where a longer ship could not.

Still the same results are found if we apply No. 4 and allow upper E all her powers of reversing and helm, in her endeavour to avoid lower E. By porting her helm, upper E only gives lower E more ample warning of her act. Her powers of reducing her way are such that starboard helm will not so certainly make collision should lower E port, unless the crossing angle is small, or the distance from the crossing-point is small. But the danger all remains, if it be not increased, should lower E continue her course. Like results follow the application of No. 5 to E (No. 1).

We have now looked at a really considerable variety of cases, probably quite enough to generalise from. If it be thought not, then the student may almost infinitely multiply them for himself. What will appear, however they are multiplied, and the more strongly the more they are multiplied, will be these .canons of the art of avoiding collision when the courses cross at right angles or less than a right angle.

Given some such plain rule as one which said—"You may cross a ship's bows leaving her on your port (or left) hand; but you must not cross a ship's bows leaving her on your starboard (or right) hand": then (1) it will always be right for you to port your helm to avoid a ship which has the right to cross your bows. (2) It will always further be right for you when you port your helm, to reduce your speed by all means in your power. (3) It will always be right for you when you port, to turn as short as your manœuvring powers will allow. (4) On approaching a ship whose bows you have the right to cross, you must always be guarded. If you have the slightest doubt whether she can, or will, permit you to exercise your right, you must instantly yield it by turning towards her, by starboarding your helm. But you must understand that you may, at any later moment, get a signal from the other ship to right your helm, which signal you must instantly obey.

Many seamen have in their minds some general conception of the truth of the foregoing, but they limit their acquiescence to certain cases, and do not even carry them over the whole field that I have now done. They generally rigidly exclude all cases when the courses cross at more than a right angle, and consider that though we may very plausibly say 'never port to a green light' and 'never starboard to a red light' if we could ensure that the crossing angle was small, yet it cannot be done because of the numerous cases where—chiefly on account of the large crossing angle—such definite instructions would be highly dangerous.

By means of these transparent diagrams, which disclose what ships really do, and not what we might suppose them to do, we are in a good position to examine all these supposititious cases.

Let us take ship E (No. 1) as before, and consider lower E steering W. as before, while upper E is steering N.W., being to port of lower E, with the crossing-point at the 9th interval for each ship. We might very readily think we had arrived at a state of things which at once broke down the whole fabric we had just built up. But is it so? These ships' bows are only 225 yards from each other. How do we suppose them to have got into that proximity? If we placed the ships as close as that, when their courses crossed at a right angle or less than a right angle, we have inevitable collision no matter what is done on either side. The least distance apart we have yet dealt with is some 400 yards, and we never brought the two E's so near as 400 yards. Neither law nor seamanship can undertake impossibilities, and if ships get within a couple of lengths of each other when movement is necessary to avoid collision, we cannot lay down rules for them, because it can only be in some very rare cases that rules can be of any avail. To be reasonable, we must suppose we are laying down rules when, in the general case, and guided by like appearances, the mariner will avoid collision by acting on them. If he allows himself to get into, or is forced into, such close proximity that in the general case nothing would save him, then we hardly undertake to say what he should do.

So let us put these two E's, the lower steering W. and the upper steering N.W., so far apart that they would in the general case have some chance of avoiding each other by a proper exercise of seamanship—say 400 yards or thereabouts. Say in fact that the 13th intervals coincide, and form the crossing-point.

Now we have conditions somewhat approaching those with which we have hitherto dealt. But even if upper E saw exactly the same appearances which we have supposed would have caused her to act in former cases, the conditions are changed, inasmuch as she has a great deal more *time* to act in. She is nearer to lower E than she ever was before, but she is nearly half as far again from the crossing-point. Here we have one of those unrecognized reasons why collisions so seldom come about out of such conditions as these. Say the night is such that you cannot see a coloured light beyond 500 yards, then the larger the crossing angle between your own course and that of the ship carrying the light seen 500 yards off, so much the more time have you to act in, and so much the greater is your power to deal with your speed.

But with these two E's there is still a good deal of difference of condition to be noticed before we set them manœuvring. Before we came to this case, neither E had seen the other more than 4 points on his bow; but these E's now see each other 6 points on the bow. This is at least a guarantee that lower E will not be disposed to alter his course. If it is at night, a green light 6 points on the bow, even if it does not materially change its bearing, will not awake any fears unless it is very close indeed. For upper E, a red light 6 points on the starboard bow, is not an immediate danger, and even if it shows no signs of changing its bearing, it does not prompt either helm, certainly not starboard helm, because of the impossibility of knowing when the course may be resumed; if starboard helm was proper, it cannot be resumed as long as the red light is there. Undoubtedly the seamanlike course is to reduce the speed without touching the helm, at least until the red light has somewhat drawn ahead.

But suppose that, abandoning all that instinctive knowledge that the seaman has about the general safety of things seen very broad on the bow, the mariner in upper E should follow the lessons taught in preceding pages, and should put his helm to port and reduce his speed—will he do anything very dangerous or improper? We see at once that even if he neglected to reduce his speed his turn would allow lower E to pass ahead of him. Of couse, as we can see by putting No. 4 in upper E's place, reducing speed makes greater safety. All the other ships are in like case.

It may here be remarked that as long as we use E No. 1 as the ship to keep her course, we do not bring against her any ship with superior speed, and that the case would be altered if we did. But the answer is, that if the giving way ship had the superior speed she would see the change of bearing—the light she observed would draw still further aft, and she would neither alter course or speed—there being no occasion for it. If, however, the two ships were equally distant from the crossing-point in time, and that therefore there was no change of bearing, then the giving-way ship with superior speed must sight the other more nearly ahead, and would be bound to port her helm and reduce her speed. Take, for instance, ship T (No. 2) steering W., and the ship E (No. 1), to port of her steering N.W., and let them each be 13 intervals from the crossing-point while they are 400 yards apart. The further conditions must be that T is only 3 points on the starboard bow of E, and the latter could not possibly strike T if she put her helm hard a-port, even if she did not reduce her speed. No doubt in this case, that E might starboard her helm with even more complete impunity. But a red light not changing its bearing three points on the bow, may just as well belong to a ship steering S.S.W. as W., and the seaman must do that which would be safest in either case.

I believe that those who have imagined that it is, as has been said, 'often' the best course to port the helm to a green light, or to starboard it to a red light, have never looked at the question closely enough. Starting with the obvious truism that if two ships are steering courses converging on one another, such as X to port steering North, and Y to starboard steering N.W., and are pretty close together, they may avoid each other by turning outwards—away from each other; they have omitted to reflect that this is not the question. This close proximity is only a necessity in narrow waters where all the circumstances of each ship are known to the other. We want rules of law and seamanship which will avoid this close proximity in the open sea, and the teacher should show how to avoid it, and not what to do when by neglect of seamanship a state of things has been brought about such as adherence to seamanship would have avoided. These transparent diagrams, for the first time in the history of this question, are capable of giving definite answers on all these points, and showing where the real seamanship lies. My hope is, that as the data contained in these diagrams is incontrovertible, and as there is plenty more of the same sort at the back of it, sound views may ultimately prevail, and even while the law still remains faulty, seamen may get to know wherein its faults lie, and not be misled by them.

APPENDIX.

REVISED REGULATIONS FOR PREVENTING COLLISIONS AT SEA, ISSUED IN PURSUANCE OF THE MERCHANT SHIPPING ACT AMENDMENT ACT, 1862. (ORDER IN COUNCIL, 11th AUG., 1884.)

Article 1. In the following rules every steam-ship which is under sail and not under steam is to be considered a sailing ship; and every steam-ship which is under steam, whether under sail or not, is to be considered a ship under steam.

Rules concerning Lights.

Article 2. The lights mentioned in the following Articles, numbered 3, 4, 5, 6, 7, 8, 9, 10, and 11, and no others, shall be carried in all weathers, from sunset to sunrise.

Article 3. A sea-going steam-ship when under way shall carry—

(*a*) On or in front of the foremast, at a height above the hull of not less than 20 feet, and if the breadth of the ship exceeds 20 feet, then at a height above the hull not less than such breadth, a bright white light, so constructed as to show an uniform and unbroken light over an arc of the horizon of 20 points of the compass, so fixed as to throw the light 10 points on each side of the ship, viz., from right ahead to two points abaft the beam on either side, and of such a character as to be visible on a dark night, with a clear atmosphere, at a distance of at least five miles.

(*b*) On the starboard side a green light, so constructed as to show an uniform and unbroken light over an arc of the horizon of 10 points of the compass, so fixed as to throw the light from right ahead to two points abaft the beam on the starboard side, and of such a character as to be visible on a dark night, with a clear atmosphere, at a distance of at least two miles.

(*c*) On the port side a red light, so constructed as to show an uniform and unbroken light over an arc of the horizon of 10 points of the compass, so fixed as to throw the light from right ahead to two points abaft the beam on the port side, and of such a character as to be visible on a dark night, with a clear atmosphere, at a distance of at least two miles.

(*d*) The said green and red side-lights shall be fitted with inboard screens projecting at least 3 feet forward from the light, so as to prevent these lights from being seen across the bow.

Article 4. A steam-ship, when towing another ship, shall, in addition to her side-lights, carry two bright white lights in a vertical line one over the other, not less than 3 feet apart, so as to distinguish her from other steam-ships. Each of these lights shall be of the same construction and character, and shall be carried in the same position, as the white light which other steam-ships are required to carry.

Article 5 (*a*) A ship, whether a steam-ship or a sailing ship, which from any accident is not under command, shall at night carry, in the same position as the white light which steam-ships are required to carry, and, if a steam-ship, in place of that light, three red lights in globular lanterns, each not less than 10 inches in diameter, in a vertical line one over the other, not less than 3 feet apart, and of such a character as to be visible on a dark night with a clear atmosphere at a distance of at least two miles; and shall by day carry in a vertical line one over the other, not less than

3 feet apart, in front of but not lower than her foremast head, three black balls or shapes, each 2 feet in diameter.

(*b*) A ship, whether a steam-ship or a sailing ship employed in laying or in picking up a telegraph cable, shall at night carry in the same position as the white light which steam-ships are required to carry, and, if a steam-ship, in place of that light, three lights in globular lanterns each not less than 10 inches in diameter, in a vertical line over one another, not less than 6 feet apart; the highest and lowest of these lights shall be red, and the middle light shall be white, and they shall be of such a character that the red lights shall be visible at the same distance as the white light. By day she shall carry in a vertical line one over the other not less than 6 feet apart, in front of but not lower than her foremast head, three shapes not less than 2 feet in diameter, of which the top and bottom shall be globular in shape and red in colour, and the middle one diamond in shape, and white.

(*c*) The ships referred to in this Article, when not making any way through the water, shall not carry the side-lights, but when making way shall carry them.

(*d*) The lights and shapes required to be shown by this Article are to be taken by other ships as signals that the ship showing them is not under command, and cannot therefore get out of the way.

Article 6. A sailing ship under way, or being towed, shall carry the same lights as are provided by Article 3 for a steam-ship under way, with the exception of the white light, which she shall never carry.

Article 7. Whenever, as in the case of small vessels during bad weather, the green and red side-lights cannot be fixed, these lights shall be kept on deck, on their respective sides of the vessel, ready for use; and shall, on the approach of or to other vessels, be exhibited on their respective sides in sufficient time to prevent collision, in such manner as to make them most visible, and so that the green light shall not be seen on the port-side, nor the red light on the starboard-side.

To make the use of these portable lights more certain and easy, the lanterns containing them shall each be painted outside with the colour of the light they respectively contain, and shall be provided with proper screens.

Article 8. A ship, whether a steam-ship or a sailing ship, when at anchor, shall carry, where it can best be seen, but at a height not exceeding 20 feet above the hull, a white light, in a globular lantern of not less than 8 inches in diameter, and so constructed as to show a clear uniform and unbroken light visible all round the horizon, at a distance of at least one mile.

Article 9. A pilot vessel, when engaged on her station on pilotage duty, shall not carry the lights required for other vessels, but shall carry a white light at the masthead, visible all round the horizon, and shall also exhibit a flare-up light or flare-up lights at short intervals, which shall never exceed fifteen minutes.

A pilot vessel, when not engaged on her station on pilotage duty, shall carry lights similar to those of other ships.

Article 10. Open boats and fishing vessels of less than 20 tons net registered tonnage, when under way and when not having their nets, trawls, dredges, or lines in the water, shall not be obliged to carry the coloured side-lights; but every such boat and vessel shall in lieu thereof have ready at hand a lantern with a green glass on the one side and a red glass on the other side, and on approaching to or being approached by another vessel such lantern shall be exhibited in sufficient time to prevent collision, so that the green light shall not be seen on the port-side, nor the red light on the starboard-side.

The following portion of this Article applies only to fishing vessels and boats when in the sea off the coast of Europe lying north of Cape Finisterre:—

(*a*) All fishing vessels and fishing boats of 20 tons net registered tonnage, or upwards, when under way and when not required by the following regulations in this Article to carry and show the lights therein named, shall carry and show the same lights as other vessels under way.

(*b*) All vessels when engaged in fishing with drift nets shall exhibit two white lights from any part of the vessel where they can be best seen. Such lights shall be placed so that the vertical distance between them shall be not less than 6 feet and not more than 10 feet; and so that the horizontal distance between them measured in a line with the keel of the vessel shall be not less than 5 feet and not more than 10 feet. The lower of these two lights shall be the more forward, and both of them shall be of such a character, and contained in lanterns of such construction as to show all round the horizon, on a dark night with a clear atmosphere, for a distance of not less than three miles.

(*c*) A vessel employed in line fishing with her lines out shall carry the same lights as a vessel when engaged when fishing with drift nets.

(*d*) If a vessel when fishing becomes stationary in consequence of her gear getting fast to a rock or other obstruction, she shall show the light and make the fog-signal for a vessel at anchor.

(*e*) Fishing vessels and open boats may at any time use a flare-up in addition to the lights which they are by this Article required to carry and show. All flare-up lights exhibited by a vessel when trawling, dredging, or fishing with any kind of drag net shall be shown at the after part of the vessel, excepting that, if the vessel is hanging by the stern to her trawl, dredge, or drag net, they shall be exhibited from the bow.

(*f*) Every fishing vessel and every open boat when at anchor between sunset and sunrise shall exhibit a white light visible all round the horizon at a distance of at least one mile.

(*g*) In fog, mist, or falling snow, a drift-net vessel attached to her nets, and a vessel when trawling, dredging, or fishing with any kind of drag net, and a vessel employed in line fishing with her lines out, shall at intervals of not more than two minutes make a blast with her fog-horn and ring her bell alternately.

Article 11. A ship which is being overtaken by another shall show from her stern to such last-mentioned ship a white light or a flare-up light.

Sound Signals for Fog, &c.

Article 12. A steam-ship shall be provided with a steam-whistle or other efficient steam sound signal, so placed that the sound may not be intercepted by any obstructions, and with an efficient fog-horn to be sounded by a bellows or other mechanical means, and also with an efficient bell.* A sailing ship shall be provided with a similar fog-horn and bell.

In fog, mist, or falling snow, whether by day or night, the signals described in this Article shall be used as follows; that is to say,—

(*a*) A steam-ship under way shall make with her steam-whistle, or other steam sound signal, at intervals of not more than two minutes, a prolonged blast.

(*b*) A sailing ship under way shall make with her fog-horn, at intervals of not more than two minutes, when on the starboard-tack one blast, when on the port-tack two blasts in succession, and when with the wind abaft the beam three blasts in succession.

(*c*) A steam-ship and a sailing ship, when not under way, shall at intervals of not more than two minutes ring the bell.

Speed of Ships to be moderate in Fog, &c.

Article 13. Every ship, whether a sailing ship or steam-ship, shall in a fog, mist, or falling snow, go at a moderate speed.

Steering and Sailing Rules.

Article 14. When two sailing ships are approaching one another, so as to involve risk of collision, one of them shall keep out of the way of the other, as follows, viz.:—

(*a*) A ship which is running free shall keep out of the way of a ship which is close-hauled.

(*b*) A ship which is close-hauled on the port-tack shall keep out of the way of a ship which is close-hauled on the starboard-tack.

* In all cases where the Regulations require a bell to be used, a drum will be substituted on board Turkish vessels.

(*c*) When both are running free with the wind on different sides, the ship which has the wind on the port-side shall keep out of the way of the other.

(*d*) When both are running free with the wind on the same side, the ship which is to windward shall keep out of the way of the ship which is to leeward.

(*e*) A ship which has the wind aft shall keep out of the way of the other ship.

Article 15. If two ships under steam are meeting end-on or nearly end-on, so as to involve risk of collision, each shall alter her course to starboard, so that each may pass on the port-side of the other.

This Article only applies to cases where ships are meeting end-on or nearly end-on, in such a manner as to involve risk of collision, and does not apply to two ships which must, if both kept on their respective courses, pass clear of each other.

The only cases to which it does apply are, when each of the two ships is end-on or nearly end-on to the other; in other words, to cases in which, by day, each ship sees the masts of the other in a line, or nearly in a line, with her own; and by night, to cases in which each ship is in such a position as to see both the side-lights of the other.

It does not apply by day to cases in which a ship sees another ahead crossing her own course; or by night to cases where the red light of one ship is opposed to the red light of the other, or where the green light of one ship is opposed to the green light of the other, or where a red light without a green light, or a green light without a red light, is seen ahead, or where both green and red lights are seen anywhere but ahead.

Article 16. If two ships under steam are crossing, so as to involve risk of collision, the ship which has the other on her own starboard-side shall keep out of the way of the other.

Article 17. If two ships, one of which is a sailing ship and the other a steam-ship, are proceeding in such direction as to involve risk of collision, the steam-ship shall keep out of the way of the sailing ship.

Article 18. Every steam-ship, when approaching another ship, so as to involve risk of collision, shall slacken her speed or stop and reverse, if necessary.

Article 19. In taking any course authorized or required by these Regulations, a steam-ship under way may indicate that course to any other ship which she has in sight by the following signals on her steam-whistle, viz. :—

One short blast to mean "I am directing my course to starboard."

Two short blasts to mean "I am directing my course to port."

Three short blasts to mean "I am going full speed astern."

The use of these signals is optional, but if they are used the course of the ship must be in accordance with the signal made.

Article 20. Notwithstanding anything contained in any preceding Article, every ship, whether a sailing ship or a steam-ship, overtaking any other shall keep out of the way of the overtaken ship.

Article 21. In narrow channels every steam-ship shall, when it is safe and practicable, keep to that side of the fairway or mid-channel which lies on the starboard-side of such ship.

Article 22. Where by the above Rules one of two ships is to keep out of the way, the other shall keep her course.

Article 23. In obeying and construing these Rules, due regard shall be had to all dangers of navigation; and to any special circumstances which may render a departure from the above Rules necessary in order to avoid immediate danger.

No Ship, under any Circumstances, to neglect Proper Precautions.

Article 24. Nothing in these Rules shall exonerate any ship, or the owner, or the master, or crew thereof, from the consequences of any neglect to carry lights or signals, or of any neglect to keep a proper look-out, or of the neglect of any precaution which may be required by the ordinary practice of seamen, or by the special circumstances of the case.

Reservation of Rules for Harbours and Inland Navigation.

Article 25. Nothing in these Rules shall interfere with the operation of a special rule duly made by local authority, relative to the navigation of any harbour, river, or inland navigation.

Special Lights for Squadrons and Convoys.

Article 26. Nothing in these Rules shall interfere with the operation of any special rules made by the Government of any nation with respect to additional station and signal-lights for two or more ships of war, or for ships sailing under convoy.

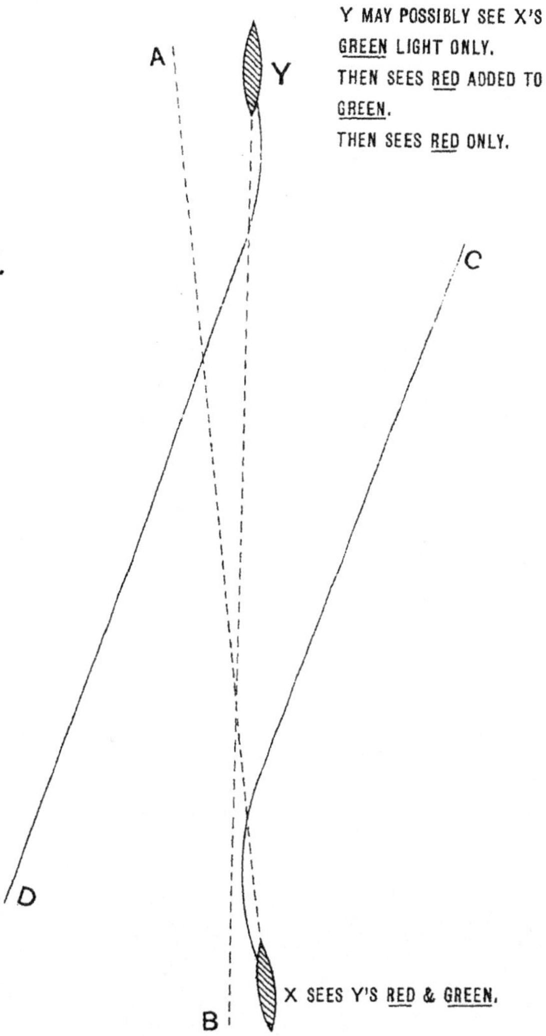

Fig. 1.

SCALE (SAY) ⅛-IN. = 100 YARDS.

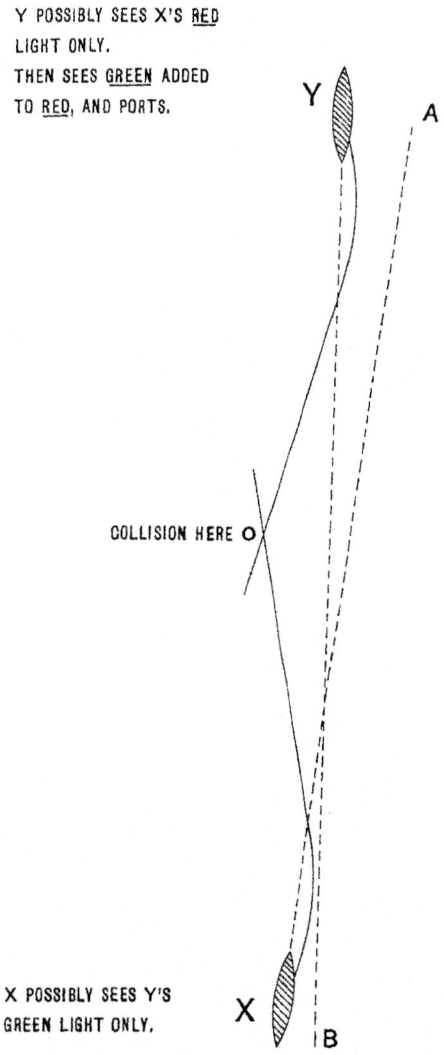

Fig. 2.

SCALE (SAY) ¼-IN. = 100 YARDS.

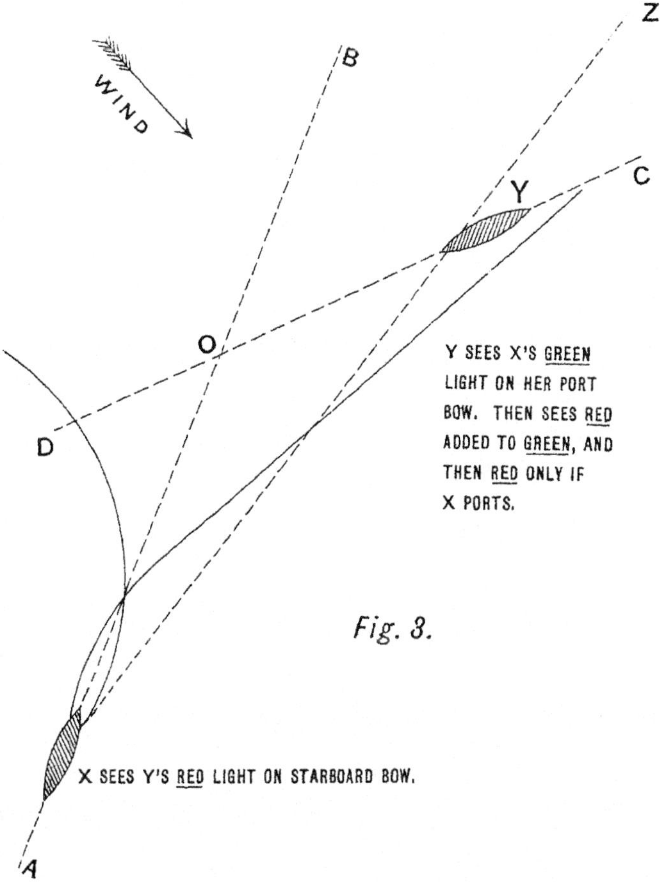
WIND
B
Z
C
Y
O
D
A
Y SEES X'S GREEN LIGHT ON HER PORT BOW. THEN SEES RED ADDED TO GREEN, AND THEN RED ONLY IF X PORTS.
X SEES Y'S RED LIGHT ON STARBOARD BOW.

Fig. 3.

Fig. 4.

SCALE 0.332-IN. = 100 FEET.

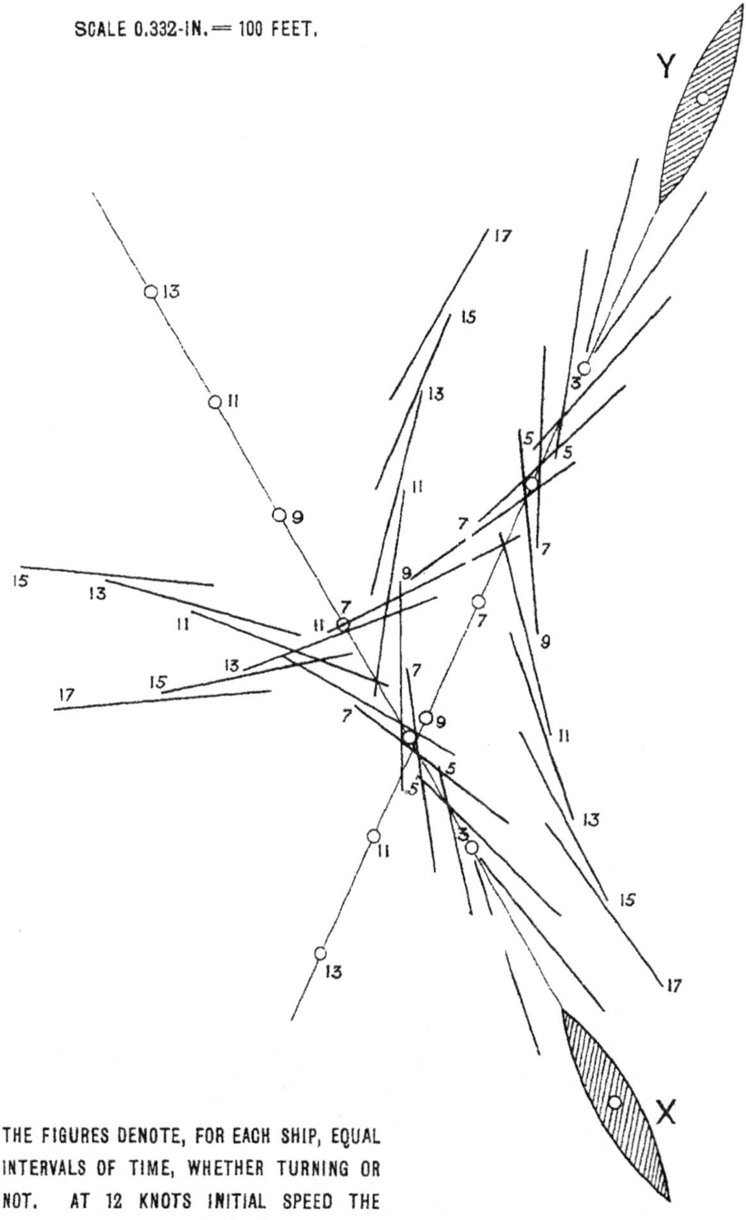

THE FIGURES DENOTE, FOR EACH SHIP, EQUAL INTERVALS OF TIME, WHETHER TURNING OR NOT. AT 12 KNOTS INITIAL SPEED THE INTERVAL IS FIVE SECONDS ON THIS SCALE.

SCALE ¼-IN. = 100 FEET.

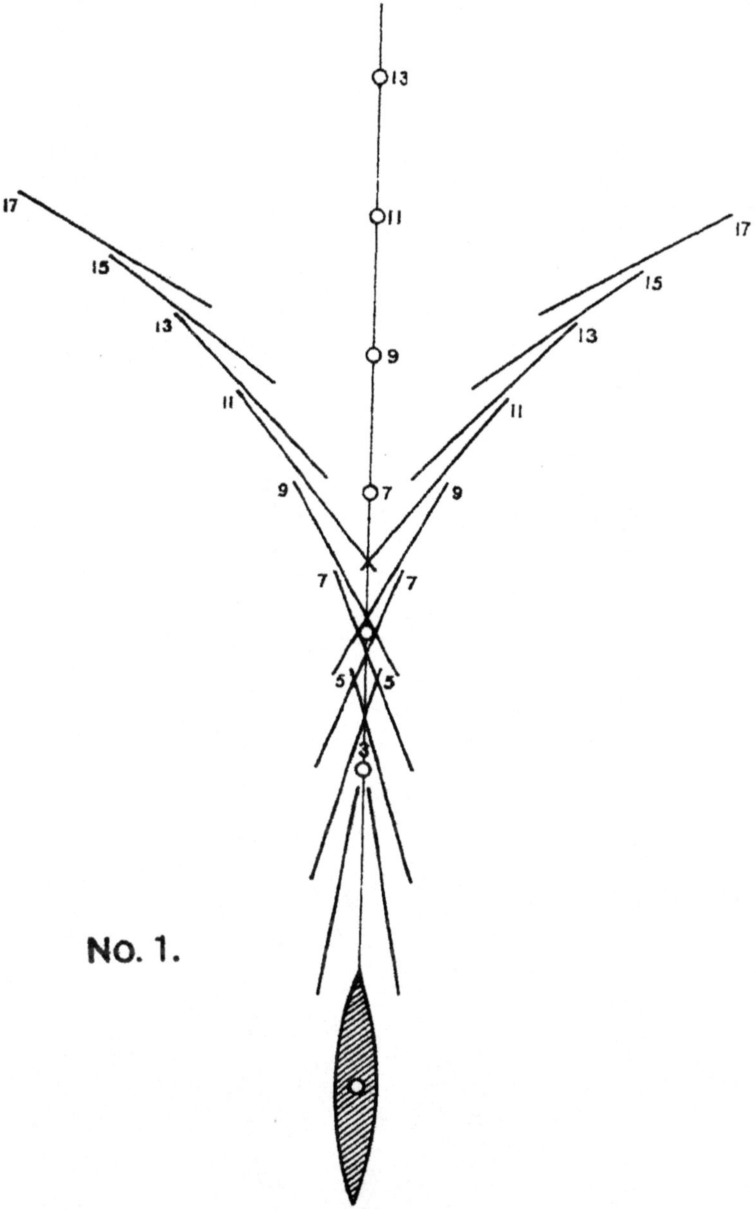

No. 1.

SHIP E. 9,000 TONS. 34° HELM.

INTERVALS = FIVE SECONDS AT 12 KNOTS.

SCALE ¼-IN. = 100-FT.

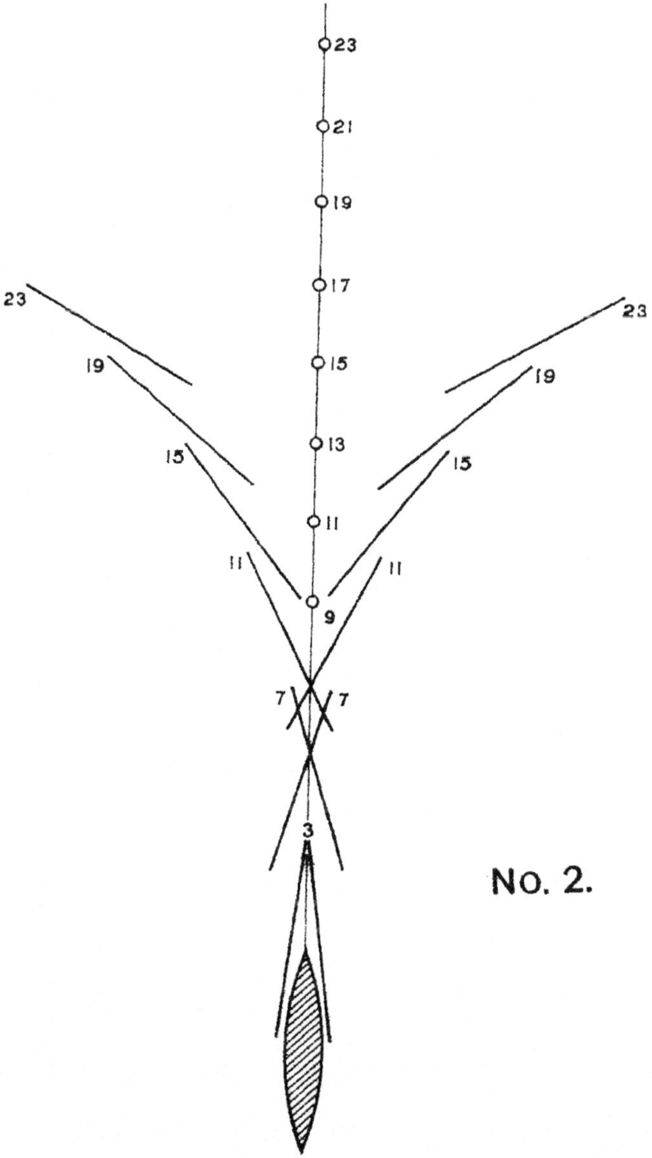

No. 2.

SHIP T. 9,000 TONS. 34° HELM.

INTERVALS = 5 SECONDS AT 6¼ KNOTS.

SCALE ½-IN. = 100 FEET.

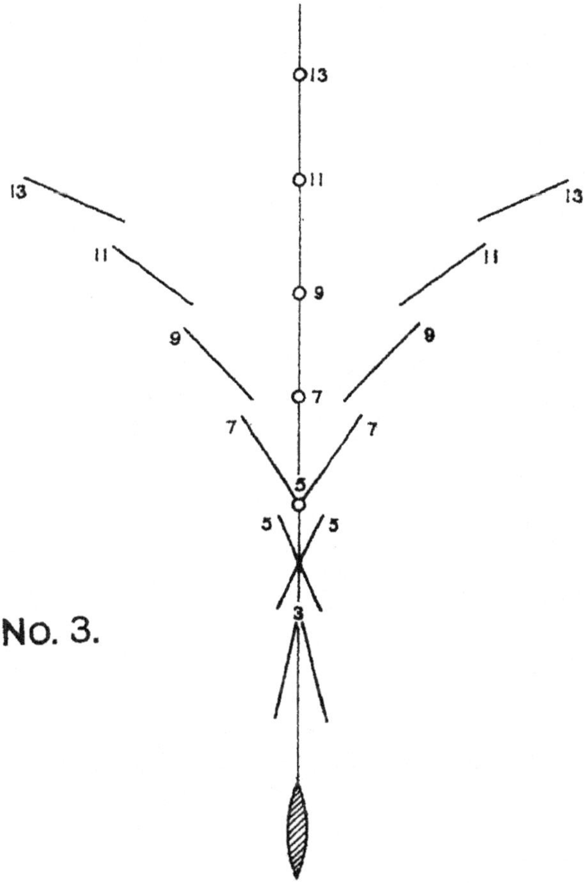

No. 3.

SHIP F. 600 TONS. 32° HELM.

INTERVALS = 5 SECONDS AT 9½ KNOTS.

SCALE ⅛-IN. = 100 FEET.

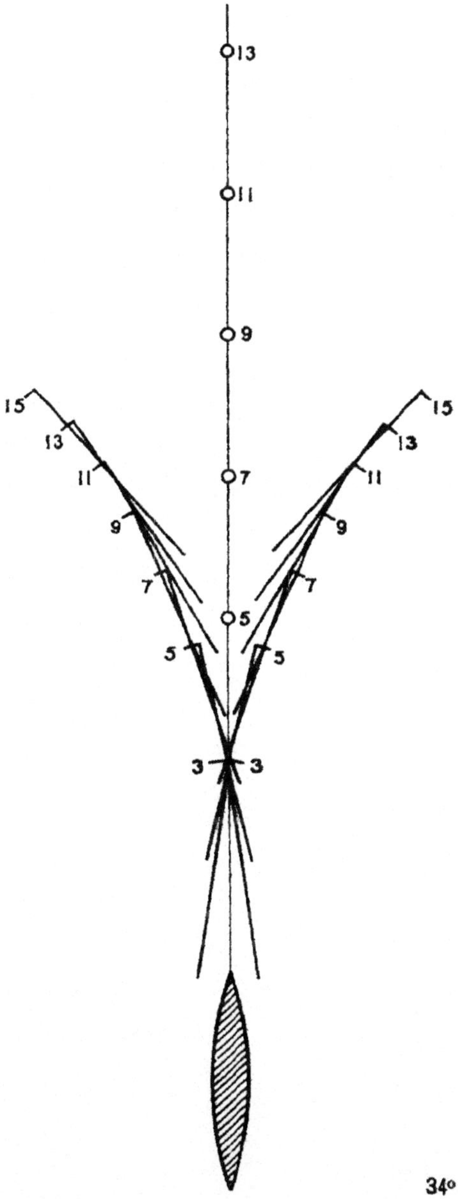

No. 4.

SHIP E. 9000 TONS.
REVERSING FULL SPEED.

34° HELM.
INTERVALS = 5 SECONDS
AT 12 KNOTS ORIGINAL SPEED.

SCALE ⅓-IN. = 100 FEET.

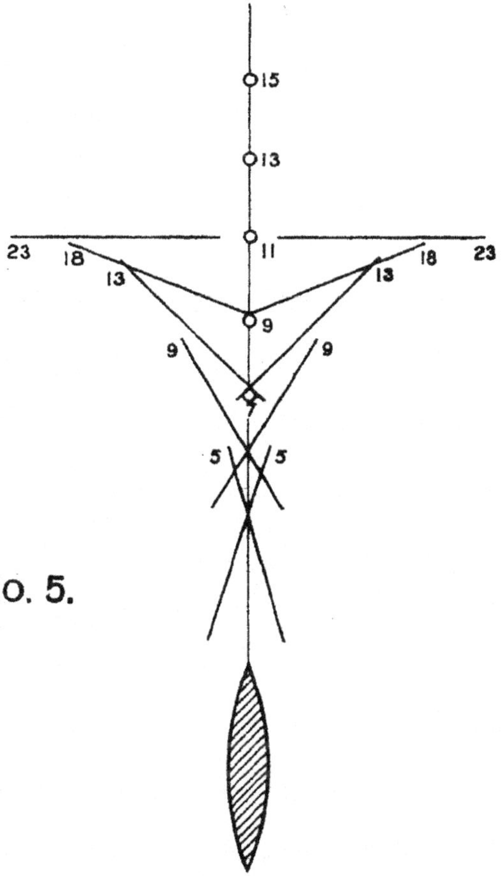

NO. 5.

SHIP T. 9,000 TONS. 34° HELM. INNER SCREW REVERSED.
INTERVALS = 5 SECONDS AT 6½ KNOTS ORIGINAL SPEED.

Printed in Dunstable, United Kingdom

91219472R00067